INUIT PEOPLES OF CANADA

PALMER PATTERSON

Grolier Limited
TORONTO

FOCUS ON CANADIAN HISTORY SERIES

SERIES CONSULTANT: DESMOND MORTON

Cover design, maps and drawings: Cheryl Trevers

Illustration credits: Public Archives of Canada, cover (PA 129589) and pages 35 (129587), 36 (C 35450), 38 (PA 114667), 42 (PA 114724), 46 (PA 102651), 49 (PA 129588), 51 (PA 114680), 57 (PA 112090), 59 (PA 129590), 60 (PA 114660), 64 (PA 114678), 67 (PA 101172), 71 (PA 129021), 73 (PA 114718); National Museums of Canada, pages 16, 18, 27, 45, 48, 52, 63, 74, 82; Metropolitan Toronto Library, page 32; Department of Indian Affairs and Northern Development, pages 77, 78; Government of the Northwest Territories, page 81.

Canadian Cataloguing in Publication Data

Patterson, E. Palmer, 1927-
   Inuit peoples of Canada

(Focus on Canadian history series)
For use in schools.
Includes index.
ISBN 0-7172-1823-6

1. Inuit—Canada.*
I. Title.   II. Series.

E99.E7P18   970.004 '97   C82-095038-6

1234567890   THB   098765432

Printed and Bound in Canada

Contents

Introduction

Canadians often refer to their country's northern location when they talk, write and sing about it. Their national anthem speaks of Canada as "the true North, strong and free." John Diefenbaker, when he was prime minister, spoke of the "vision of the North." The North and northernness are part of Canadians' image of themselves and their country: free, strong, open, natural, beautiful, vast and challenging.

Yet the great majority of Canadians live in a relatively narrow strip along the country's southern border. Few of them—indeed few people anywhere—have more than a vague idea based on their own experience of winter what the vast frozen lands of the Arctic are really like. They mistakenly picture them as being always cold and dreary and therefore unpleasant. They do not give much thought to the practical implications of living in such a land—especially without the resources of modern technology.

The Land
Geographically, the Canadian North presents a wide variety of landscapes. The islands of the High Arctic are mountainous, their shorelines indented by deep fiords. South of the major islands lies the area known as the Barren Grounds, a vast rolling plain that stretches from the west coast of Hudson Bay to Great Slave Lake. West of this is the Mackenzie River delta, a low-lying area dotted with *pingos*—small cone-shaped hills with a core of solid ice. To the east, the interior of northern Quebec is very similar to the Barren Grounds. Labrador for the most part is rocky, rugged and bleak.

For nine months of the year, the Canadian Arctic is as most southerners imagine it—a featureless, windswept, snow-covered desert. The Arctic seas, lakes and rivers freeze solid by October and stay that way until June. Temperatures may fall below -55°C. In midwinter, there is no daylight for weeks north of the Arctic circle, only a brief twilight at midday. Earlier and later, and in more southerly regions, when the sun does rise above the horizon, the glare of its reflection on the snow is literally blinding. And when the sky is overcast it sometimes merges with the horizon and the snow-covered ground into a shimmering, shadowless, endless whiteness, in which distance and direction become impossible to judge.

But even in the Far North, winter does not last forever, and the Arctic summer is filled with life and colour. The days are long and cloudless, and for a while at midsummer the sun never sets. The temperature rises above freezing, the top layer of soil thaws, and hundreds of different kinds of plants spring to life. Over two thousand kinds of lichen appear in colours of purple, orange, red, green, yellow and white. Flowers burst into bloom—arctic crocus, white heather, purple saxifrage, cress, arctic poppy, rhododendron, lousewort and many, many others.

Although we speak of the "treeline" and define the tundra as "treeless," several kinds of tree do grow there, including arctic willow, birch and alder. But they grow slowly and never large, staying close to the earth for warmth, moisture and nourishment. A tree may be over a hundred years old and less than a metre high, with its trunk no larger than a man's thumb.

A variety of animals feed on this vegetation. Once they did so in even greater numbers. Years of overhunting have threatened the existence of some, and wildlife sanctuaries have been created to protect them. In the Thelon Game Sanctuary can be found musk-ox, caribou, arctic fox, the rare arctic wolf, arctic hare, moose, lemming and grizzly bear. Bird sanctuaries containing marshes and shallow lakes and ponds provide nesting areas for

---

The lands north of the tree line have traditionally been considered Inuit territory.

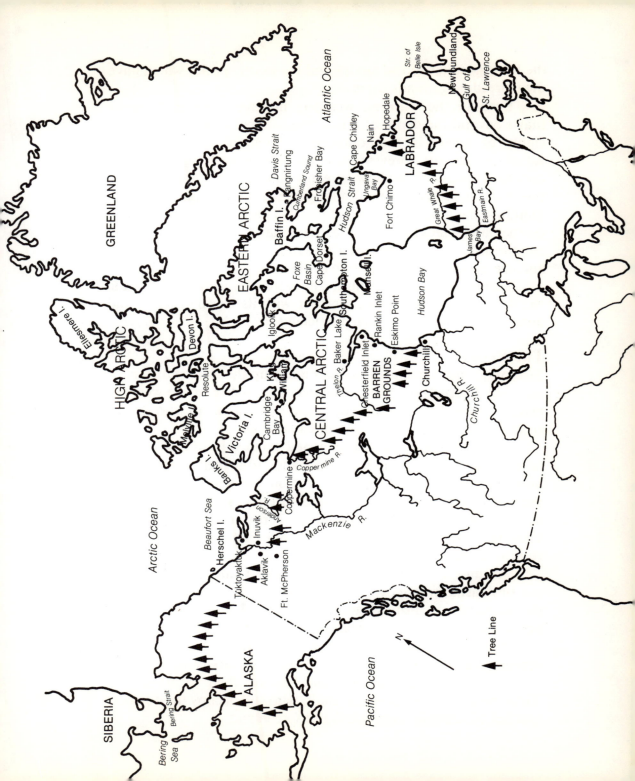

the birds peculiar to the tundra and the many species which have their breeding grounds there.

Even in the warmest weather, however, the earth never thaws beyond the depth of a few centimetres, maybe as many as eighty or ninety in the southernmost region. This condition, called permafrost, prevents the run-off of melting snow and creates a maze of shallow streams and ponds. Soil develops poorly in such conditions, limiting the growth of plant life and therefore the amount of animal life that can be supported. Mosquitoes and blackflies, on the other hand, thrive in such wet conditions and breed by the thousands to plague both animals and the people who live in this harsh land.

Those people are the Inuit. The extreme northern part of the North American continent, together with its nearby islands and northeastern Siberia, is their homeland.

The People

Two major movements of peoples make up the history of the Inuit ("the People") in Arctic Canada. The first to arrive were the people of the Arctic Small Tool Tradition—a group who moved from Alaska about four thousand years ago.

These people gradually changed their way of life as they adapted to their new environment, and from their adaptation a new culture developed *in situ*, or "on the spot"—the Dorset culture. The Dorset people's way of life focussed mainly on the seal and was remarkably similar all across the vast stretch of Canada's Arctic. It survived in northern Canada until at least a thousand years ago.

Around A.D. 1000, a new people, the Thule, began to move out of Alaska, where there had been a long, varied, and complex development of cultures and peoples. The Thule quickly spread across northern Canada, replacing or absorbing the Dorset.

The Thule were whale hunters. However, in the seventeenth century climatic changes forced them to diversify and turn to various other food sources depending on their location. The Thule people then became the Inuit, who still occupy the northern reaches of Canada from Alaska to Greenland.

With the coming of the Vikings and later European explorers new elements began to be introduced into the Inuit way of life. In the nineteenth century European and American whalers appeared, first in the eastern then in the western Arctic. Their arrival created still more, and more lasting, change. The Inuit came to depend on goods brought in by these outsiders. Widespreading epidemic diseases were introduced, and the native population suffered sharp declines.

By the early twentieth century, whaling had ceased to dominate the Inuit economy, though it did continue locally. Fur trading, especially for white fox furs, became the means by which the Inuit obtained the manufactured goods they needed. But in the 1930s, the fur trade too declined. World War II and the "Cold War" brought construction in the North, and once again the Inuit adapted. Many took work as unskilled and semi-skilled labourers. The construction boom unfortunately proved even shorter-lived than the whaling and fur-trading eras. The 1960s and 1970s saw increased native population, decreased wildlife, settlement in towns, government controls and rising unemployment. The need to create a diversity of jobs in the North was becoming apparent.

By this time more and more Inuit were organizing in order to have a voice in the changes they were experiencing, and greater control of their own future. Increasingly, they began to enter political life at the local, territorial and federal levels. A renewed cultural vigour, which manifested itself particularly in the form of art, accompanied the new upsurge in Inuit participation in public affairs.

The Inuit have always fascinated more southerly people, who marvel at their adaptation to the harsh climate and geography of the Arctic and its seeming lack of usable resources. Yet for the most part, the outside world's interest rarely led beyond a superficial picture of Inuit life based on a few colourful (and sometimes misleading) details. It is only in the past few decades that most non-Inuit have become aware of the variety, character and depth of the culture developed over thousands of years by the Inuit, their ancestors and their predecessors.

The First True Northerners: Pre-Dorset and Dorset Peoples

Evidence suggests that the earliest Inuit, like the ancestors of the Indians, came into North America across the Bering Strait from northeast Asia. They arrived much later than the Indians, however—probably no more than five or six thousand years ago—and settled in the coastal region of northwest Alaska. Between 3000 and 2000 B.C., some of these people moved eastward out of Alaska into northern Canada.

The Pre-Dorset Period—About 2500 to 800 B.C.

Archaeologists, that is scientists who specialize in the study of ancient peoples, call the first inhabitants of the Canadian Arctic the people of the Arctic Small Tool tradition. The name comes from the people's use of tiny stone tools, especially chipped flint blades. Larger chipped stones were also used, mainly for lances and spears. Stone harpoon heads were used for hunting seal and walrus.

The Arctic Small Tool people were not very numerous. They lived in small nomadic bands of one or two families, moving according to the seasons. By about 2000 B.C. they had spread to Mansell Island, northwestern Quebec and as far east as northeastern Greenland.

Before 1500 B.C. Arctic Canada was warmer than it is today.

This map shows the extent of the territory that the Pre-Dorset people are thought to have eventually occupied.

10

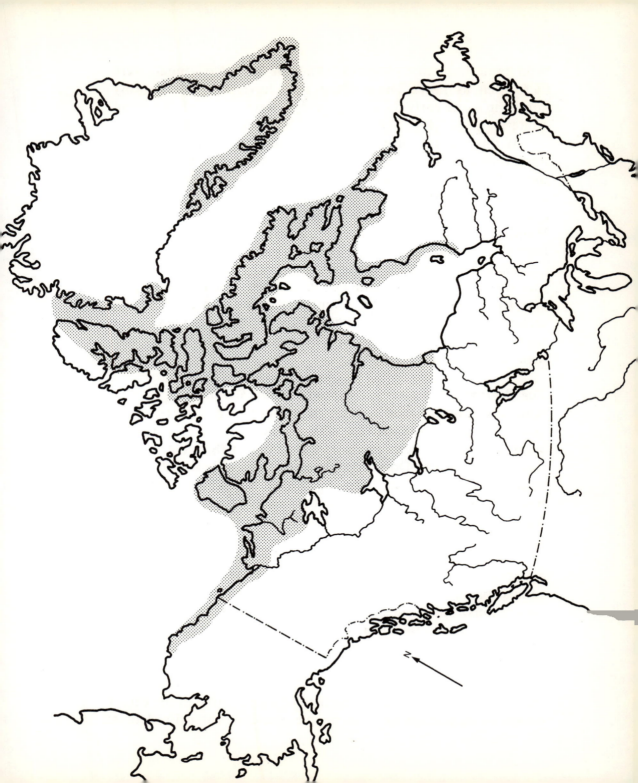

Wild game was more plentiful, although the same animals were there then as now. The animals may have been more easily hunted in those early days because they were not used to human hunters.

If this was the case, it may have encouraged the people to think that animals willingly sacrificed themselves as food for the survival of humans. Such a view would contribute to a special appreciation of the animal. It might lead to extra care and etiquette in the hunting, killing and eating of the game taken. Hunting was not always successful, however. It is likely that, from time to time, individuals or small bands died of starvation.

Box-shaped hearths made of stone slabs and gravel identify sites where Arctic Small Tool people camped. Some of these sites date from 2000 to 1700 B.C. Campsites found along beaches by archaeologists suggest that some groups probably hunted on the sea ice. The camps appear to have been occupied only briefly, and then not reoccupied.

The Beginnings of Change—About 1700 to 800 B.C.

Some areas were richer in game than others and attracted more hunters. In the period between 1700 and 800 B.C., there were such areas around northern Hudson Bay, Hudson Strait and Foxe Basin. Here the Pre-Dorset people could find caribou, fish, birds, ringed and bearded seal, harp seal, walrus and whale. The richer resources allowed for larger numbers to live together in certain seasons. They gathered at fishing sites, caribou crossings and seal and walrus hunting grounds.

In these areas, the sites found by archaeologists are larger and more numerous. They contain more artifacts. The remains of camps are clustered together and suggest seasonal use over several generations. Small sites are rare. Instead, there are remains of several structures in an area. These remains consist mainly of boulders used to hold tent edges down and left behind when the people moved on. They indicate that the dwellings were oval to circular. Interior fires were used for heating and cooking, but there were no "stone-box" hearths like those found in the earlier camps of Arctic Small Tool people. Instead, these Pre-Dorset people made lamps from soapstone, a soft stone, and burned oil extracted from seal fat, or blubber.

The Pre-Dorset lived in tents only in the summer. Their winter housing consisted of domed snowhouses built on the sea ice. These houses made it possible for them to live by hunting seal, the main winter resource.

Pre-Dorset people may have had boats of the kayak type and are known to have had the bow and arrow. Harpoons, however, were the most important tool/weapon used by these early hunters of Arctic Canada.

Harpoons are important to archaeologists as well. In particular, changes in the style of harpoons from area to area or generation to generation help them to reconstruct the lifestyles of the Pre-Dorset people. The socketed, toggling harpoon head used by the eastern Pre-Dorset people, for instance, resembles that of the Archaic Indians of Labrador. It is thought that the Pre-Dorset people may have borrowed it from the Indians while introducing them to the bow and arrow.

In the central Arctic, the Pre-Dorset hunted land mammals such as the musk-ox and caribou. They also fished for char. The people lived in small bands and returned to their camping sites over several generations. Their pattern of life was probably not much different from that followed by some Inuit of the past two or three centuries.

The Barren Grounds became Pre-Dorset hunting territory about 1700 B.C., when they were no longer used by Indians. (From about 6000 B.C. to about 1700 B.C., the Indians hunted caribou in the Barren Grounds during the summers.) In this area the people hunted seal during the milder months. In the winter they followed the caribou south into the interior. They stopped doing this after about 800 B.C., perhaps because the caribou were no longer dependable.

By about 800 to 600 B.C., the Pre-Dorset people were changing into the Dorset people.

Dorset People—about 800 B.C. to about A.D. 1000

The Dorset culture developed from the Pre-Dorset in the region

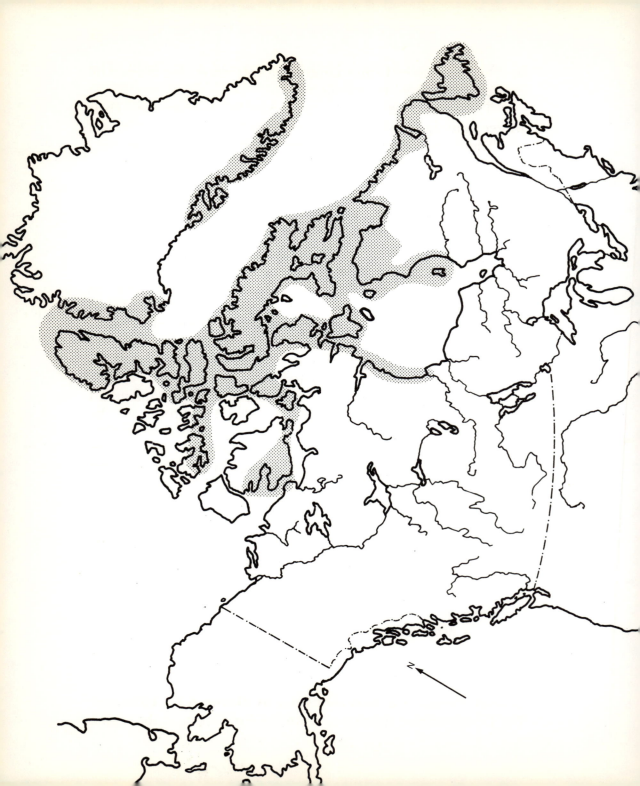

of northern Hudson Bay, Hudson Strait and Foxe Basin. The name *Dorset* was first used by anthropologist Diamond Jenness of the National Museum of Man in Ottawa. It came from artifacts found by Jenness in 1925 at Cape Dorset, on southern Baffin Island. The Dorset were called the *Tunit* by the people who later displaced them, the Thule.

The Lifestyle of the Dorset

Dorset culture emerged during a period of cooling temperature. It is richer than Pre-Dorset, with more people and more artifacts. The seasonal round of activities was linked to the peoples' food needs. In the spring and summer, they hunted for the large sea mammals—walrus and seal—in open water off the coasts. By late summer they would turn to fishing at sites known to be rich in resources, especially char. The fall and winter were spent on the coasts, where the people could hunt for seals through the ice and eat food stored from the hunting earlier in the year. Caribou, birds and small game were hunted in the spring and summer.

The Dorset used adzes, bone needles, and chipped flint and rubbed slate tools. They do not seem to have used bows and arrows, but barbed lances and toggling harpoons were very important tools in their quest for food. They are known to have had kayaks and small sleds. Dog sledding, however, is not indicated by the findings.

Dorset winter houses were built partly underground. Sometimes referred to as "longhouses," they were rectangular in shape and were occupied by two or four families. They contained rows of hearths and were lighted by blubber lamps. In the summer, the Dorset, like the Pre-Dorset, lived in skin tents.

Living as small bands of hunters, the Dorset moved with the seasons and were thinly scattered over a vast area. Their geographical distribution was different from that of the Pre-Dorset.

Map showing the territory probably occupied by the Dorset. Not all areas were occupied at the same time. The Dorset are thought to have reached Newfoundland between 500 B.C. and A.D. 500.

Most Dorset carvings were very small. For example, this pair of ivory swans found on Mansell Island is only six centimetres long. Also typical is the "X-ray" motif— fine lines carved into the ivory suggesting the birds' bones.

The Dorset extended as far west as Melville Island and as far east as Greenland. They occupied the coast of Labrador at Nain by about 700 B.C. and had extended to the southwest corner of Newfoundland by sometime between 500 B.C. and A.D. 500. They were also located on the east shore of Hudson Bay and on the west shore north of Chesterfield Inlet.

Old Dorset campsites on Ellesmere Island have risen as glaciers which had pushed the land down receded. These campsites were once located on gravel beaches and were occupied by Dorset hunters of sea mammals. Now they are inland, sometimes nearly half a kilometre from the sea.

The central Arctic was occupied by the Dorset in two migrations from the "core" area where they had first developed from Pre-Dorset. The first wave of occupation took place after 500 B.C. and ended about A.D. 100. The area was later reoccupied, but not until between A.D. 500 and 1000. The Far North was also occupied between A.D. 500 and 1000.

Archaeological evidence shows that different regions were

occupied at different times. The information available does not make clear, however, whether there were regional sub-groups and tribal variations among the Dorset. We do know that the Dorset were well adapted to the coastal tundra. They successfully hunted seal, walrus, beluga, narwhal, caribou, musk-ox, arctic hare, fox and polar bear.

A particularly rich supply of food for Dorset, and later peoples, came as a result of an odd natural phenomenon called a *polynya*. A polynya is an early melting of the sea ice. This melting brings in large numbers of animals, who come to feed. Polynya may return annually for hundreds or thousands of years and provide an abundant food source each year. Flagler Bay, near Knud Peninsula on Ellesmere Island, is one such polynya.

Art and Religious Beliefs of the Dorset

The Dorset are not the immediate ancestors of today's Inuit. However, some of what we know about them is determined from the study of more recent northern peoples. This is the case particularly in interpreting Dorset carvings. Dorset hunters made bone and ivory carvings of the animals they hunted. Based on what is known of Inuit customs, it is thought that these artfully made replicas may have been offered to animal spirits to preserve good relations between the hunter and the game hunted.

The Dorset, like the later Inuit, appear to have believed that everything in nature had a soul, or spirit. Good relations with the spirit world were considered essential not only in hunting but in any and every sphere of human endeavour. Amulets were probably used to obtain help in all the activities of the Dorset's daily life. The bear was among the most powerful creatures of the spirit world, and its image was widely distributed.

One of the traits of Dorset carvings that suggests their magical or supernatural purpose is called the *X-ray motif*. The carved animal figures have marks cut into them which suggest bones and joints—as if the inside of the animal could be seen from the outside.

Like other elements of Dorset culture, Dorset art was very much the same throughout the vast area the people occupied. The

specimens are similar wherever they are found and whether they are humans, bears, seals, birds or other animals. Wood was prominently used in Dorset art, and some specimens have been found coloured with red ochre, a pigment made from natural sources and usually associated with magical purposes.

Many carvings may have been the work of shamans, who were medicine men and women, healers, messengers and travellers to the supernatural world. The shamans were the people who had the strongest and most effective contacts with the spirits.

Archaeologists believe that life-size wood face masks that they have found were used by shamans in some of their ceremonial activities. These faces have expressions of strong emotional power carved into them. One of the archaeologists who discovered such masks reported that he felt he had looked into the face of a living Dorset shaman.

Shamans relied upon and cultivated spirit helpers—supernatural beings or "guardian angels"—through the use of secret formulas, charms and songs. Spirit helpers were thought to increase the shamans' healing powers and help them see clearly into the future. Shamans also used charms and ritual images to ward off evil spirits which opposed them and their purposes.

Most Dorset art, then, is concerned with the supernatural—but perhaps not all. Recently archaeologists have found some small stone figures of animals which do not have x-ray lines and which have a more playful look.

Decline of the Dorset

Dorset culture developed during a period when generally temperatures were falling. About A.D. 1000 there was a reversal of this condition. The Arctic began to get warmer, and Dorset culture declined. Perhaps the warmer weather caused a change in the plants and animals that were available. Also, by about this

---

Although this wooden Dorset mask is about 1000 years old, it still shows traces of the red ochre with which it was painted. It was probably made by a shaman for use in religious ceremonies. The wooden pins along the edges may have served to attach the mask to the shaman's parka hood.

time, immigration from the West had brought in the ancestors of the Inuit, the Thule.

Probably some of the Dorset were killed as a result of clashes between the two peoples. Other Dorset groups may have been pushed to marginal areas, where they could not find enough food to survive. Thule legends tell of giant Tunit (Dorset) seal hunters being driven off. Some Dorset people may have survived until well after A.D. 1000, perhaps as late as the year 1400 in the Far North and on the east coast of Hudson Bay. One small group that was still on Southampton Island in the nineteenth century is thought by some to be a last remnant of the Dorset.

In some areas, the Dorset were probably absorbed by their successors and co-existed with them for a time. Dorset artifacts are found in Thule sites, and there are Thule carvings which show women's hairstyles that were possibly borrowed from Dorset. The modern Inuit have oral traditions that tell of the Tunit (Dorset). Some of these are tales and legends. Others are more factual accounts that agree closely with archaeological evidence.

The First Inuit: Thule People—About A.D. 1000 to 1600

Chapter **2**

The ancient Greeks referred to the northernmost region they had heard of as Thule. From this Greek term comes the word that scholars of Arctic culture and history use to refer to the direct ancestors of modern Inuit. Both the people and culture are called Thule.

The Thule were most likely the earliest Inuit people to meet Europeans. It is necessary to add the phrase "most likely" because as research and discovery continue, the dates for European presence in North America may be pushed back into more remote times.

The Lifestyle of the Thule

Thule culture developed from origins in Alaska and spread eastward during a period of warming temperatures about the tenth and eleventh centuries A.D.

In particular, Thule culture grew from the Arctic whale-hunting tradition of the Bering Sea area, which was based on cultures extending back two thousand years or more in that area.

The Thule spread throughout all of the Arctic except for the extreme northwestern islands. Moreover, there was a general uniformity of Thule culture from Alaska to Greenland, which suggests that it moved rapidly across the top of North America, without time to modify and develop local variety. This rapid movement eastward was made possible by the techniques the Thule developed for hunting sea mammals—whale, walrus, seal. Whale hunting in particular was central to the Thule way of life.

21

The Thule hunted three kinds of whale: the bowhead whale, the right whale and the Greenland whale. Their most important hunting weapon was their distinctive harpoon head. An early Thule harpoon head from the Ellesmere Island region resembles closely those of the Bering Sea area. This resemblance indicates the close cultural links of the Thule throughout the Arctic.

The Thule lived in small communities or villages consisting of from one to thirty houses. Their summer dwellings were tents made from skins, but their winter houses were more substantial. These were more or less oval in shape and dug partly into the ground. The floor was paved with flat stones, and the walls were made of stones or whale bones and covered with sod. Whale ribs and jawbones were also used for rafters, and the roof was of skins. A long narrow entrance way, also dug into the ground and so low it could only be entered on hands and knees, trapped warm air inside the houses. Houses such as this have been excavated on and near Ellesmere Island where the Thule Inuit flourished for about seven hundred years. They were more permanent than those of the Dorset, and the Thule returned to the same winter sites year after year. When the sites are uncovered and exposed to the sun, they have been found to contain whale blubber, walrus gut, and rotting sinews and bones. Utensils of wood, baleen (fibrous material from the whale), ivory and bone have been excavated after being frozen for centuries.

For transportation, the Thule used dog-drawn sleds and two types of boats. The smaller single-person boat, the kayak, was made of skin, usually sealskin, stretched over a light frame of wood or bone. It was completely enclosed except for an opening in the top just big enough for one person. When occupied, the kayak was water-tight. It was used mainly for hunting seal and walrus. The other type of boat, the umiak, was much larger and open. It was used for moving people and goods from place to place and for whale hunting. Both of these types of boats were used until recently by the Inuit and are still frequently portrayed

A ENTRANCE TUNNEL
B SLEEPING PLATFORM
C COOKING AREA
D OUTSIDE WALL
E INSIDE WALL

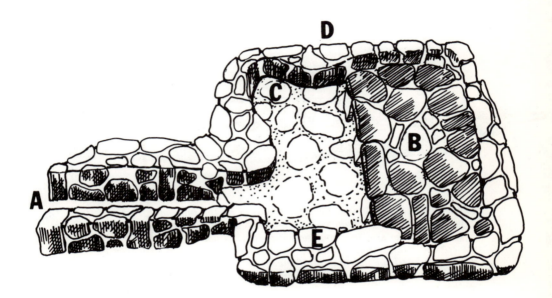

Floor plan

Floor plan of a Thule winter house showing the raised stone sleeping platform at the rear, the cooking area and the entrance tunnel.

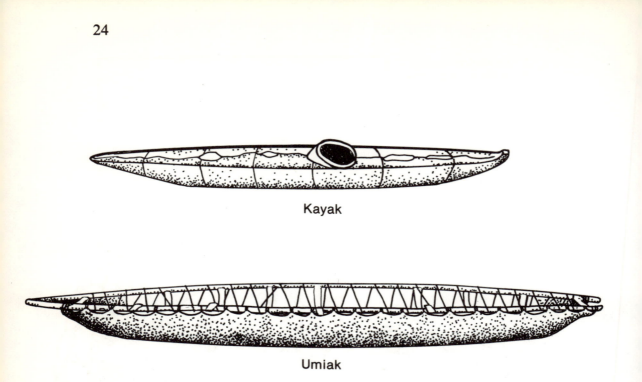

Kayak

Umiak

The kayak and umiak were used for centuries by the Inuit and their ancestors. The kayak was primarily a hunting boat and was usually between three and six metres long. The hunter's water-proof sealskin jacket could be tied around the ridge of the cockpit so that even if the kayak overturned, water would not get in. The umiak was used for transporting families and their belongings as well as for whaling. It would be between nine and twelve metres long and could carry as many as thirty people.

in contemporary Inuit art. Like the kayak, the umiak was made by stretching skins over a framework, most commonly made of driftwood. Both the kayak and the umiak were very seaworthy but could be repaired without difficulty.

Although the Thule hunted all Arctic sea mammals, the whale was particularly useful to them. As we have seen, they used the bones for building houses and boats. Whale and seal blubber was the main fuel in a land where wood was scarce. Baleen was used for beaters (to remove ice from clothes) and for drying racks and bows. The food supplied by one bowhead whale would last several families all winter.

In addition to sea mammals, the Thule hunted caribou,

From the days of the Pre-Dorset, the people of the North used large soapstone lamps to light their houses, cook food and provide some warmth. These lamps burned seal or whale oil, in some cases caribou tallow, by means of a long wick laid horizontally along the edge of the lamp.

musk-ox, polar bear, rabbit and a variety of birds. Fishing was another means of obtaining food. Skins were used for clothing, mittens and footwear, as well as for tent coverings.

When the Thule moved eastward about A.D. 1000, they took with them some pottery, which they used for lamps. However, pottery making apparently became too difficult in their new locations. Most often, proper clays were not available, and in any case, firewood was too limited to be used for firing clay. The Thule, therefore, like the Dorset, turned to using soapstone for lamps.

Some eastern Thule made implements of meteoric iron taken from northwest Greenland. (The source of the iron can be traced by analyzing the nickel content.) Several of these iron implements have been found in Thule sites on Ellesmere Island.

The leader in a Thule community or village was an older man who was a skilful and experienced hunter. He knew the best methods and places for hunting and was aided by his good connections with the beings of the supernatural world. His carefully cultivated religious and ceremonial life was important in making him successful as a hunter, and therefore acceptable as a leader.

His ability to resolve community conflicts and reduce tensions was also linked to his prestige as a successful provider.

When food was abundant, population expanded, contributing to the distribution of the Thule people across the vast Arctic region. New villages were formed when some families split off from their original band. With the aid of the dog sled, kayak and umiak, the Thule were a mobile and widely spread population.

Thule Art

Artifacts show that the Thule had a variety of tools and utensils which helped them to attain a higher standard of living than the Dorset. By comparison with the superb carvings found in Dorset sites, however, much Thule art is less distinguished and less interesting as art. One of the tools used by the Thule but unknown to the Dorset was the drill. In addition to its practical uses, the drill helped make Thule art look different from that of the Dorset.

Both Dorset and Thule carved with hard, sharp-edged stone. A very fine pointed stone can be used to gouge out small holes for the eyes of an animal figure or a mask. But only a drill can make a perfectly circular dot or hole, and then surround it with another exact circle. Not only are drilled patterns more precise, they are also faster to make. The Thule had a habit of drilling dots and circles over and over again. This repetition tends to make their carvings look less exciting. Of course, many Thule animal figures were used simply for playing games. They were not intended to call upon supernatural power but only to amuse the players.

Not all Thule art, however, is simple or repetitive. Some of it is quite interesting. A number of carvings of women and men show the decorated borders and embroidered areas of their clothing in great detail. Other artifacts have little pictures showing lively scenes of daily life incised on (cut into) bone surfaces. One of these scenes includes skin-covered houses, umiaks, kayaks, hunters with bows and arrows, whale and deer. The Thule also made dolls and large combs.

This man is using a bow drill to make a hole through a piece of bone. By holding the shaft in his mouth, he keeps his hands free to operate the bow and steady the piece he is working on.

In winter seals were hunted at their breathing holes in the ice. This required enormous amounts of patience and stamina as there was no way for the hunter to know when the seal would appear at a given hole. He might have to wait for hours, completely motionless but ready to strike instantly. In spring the hunter sometimes stalked the seals as they basked in the sun on the ice, creeping up slowly and silently until he was near enough to throw his harpoon. Or, if there was open water, he might harpoon a seal from the ice edge and retrieve it in his kayak. In summer he hunted from the kayak itself on the open water.

Some Thule carvings are very puzzling. They show groups of figures with their feet attached to barrel-shaped forms. These may have been worn by people, hung on a thong around the neck.

Thule art is generally lively and amusing to today's viewers, while Dorset art suggests supernatural power and magic. Of course, it is not possible to be certain that these are the impressions that the artists intended to produce.

The Thule Meet the Vikings

The Thule were probably the first Arctic people to meet Europeans. The Vikings, or Norsemen, arrived in Greenland in the late tenth century. About 986 Eric the Red founded two Viking settlements in southern Greenland. Another Viking settlement was established at the northwest tip of Newfoundland, at L'Anse aux Meadows. The Vikings called the Thule *skraelings*.

Viking expeditions, starting from the settlements in southern Greenland, may have reached the Ellesmere Island area by A.D. 1150. At a site near Ellesmere Island, archaeologists have discovered Viking artifacts. These include boat rivets and chain mail. Also found was a Thule-style carving about five centimetres high. In appearance and clothing the subject of the carving resembles a Viking. Other finds in the area include woollen clothes and parts of wooden barrels. These artifacts have been dated between the late twelfth and the late fourteenth centuries. They are the most northerly finds of Norse material known.

Thule Culture Begins to Change

The Viking settlements in Greenland lasted about 500 years, until 1500 or so. Those of Newfoundland ceased to exist after a much briefer span. During the years which followed, there were likely occasional encounters between the Thule and European fishermen off the east coast and among the islands, including Newfoundland. It would, however, be several hundred more years before the inhabitants of the Canadian Arctic had significant contact with Europeans. Meanwhile the Thule continued to show their remarkable ability to adapt and change to suit new conditions. Around the thirteenth century, temperatures in the Arctic began falling again. Glaciers advanced and the tree line retreated southward. This period, known as the "Little Ice Age," reached its peak between about 1600 and 1850.

During the "Little Ice Age," whales were no longer as available as in previous centuries. They could no longer constitute the Thule's main source of food and other necessities. Some people moved away. The Thule of Ellesmere Island, for example, migrated to northwest Greenland about 1700, joining Thule already resident there. Those who stayed were obliged to shift to a more mixed food base. They did more fishing and began to rely more on caribou and musk-ox. They took ringed seals at breathing holes in the ice over the water. Whereas the Thule way of life had previously been fairly uniform across the Arctic, it now began to develop regional variations as a result of adjustment to the differing conditions of different areas.

Thule and Europeans during the "Age of Discovery"

As the Thule culture was in the process of evolving into what we call the Inuit culture, Europeans arrived once again. A new surge of European exploration began in the late fifteenth century with Vasco da Gama, Bartholomew Diaz, Christopher Columbus and John Cabot. This period has been called the "Age of Discovery." It continued into the next centuries and brought European ships and people to Arctic waters in increasing numbers.

In the late sixteenth century, Martin Frobisher, an Englishman, led three expeditions into northeastern Canadian waters. He was looking for a short northern route to China, the long-dreamed of "Northwest Passage."

Thule people or their descendants met Frobisher and his men in 1576 and 1577. One of the officers under Frobisher's command gave a description of the Inuit who were met in 1576. They looked like Tartars (people of central Asia), he thought. They had long black hair, broad faces, flat noses and tan-coloured

---

This map shows the territory probably occupied by the Thule. They moved eastward out of Alaska around A.D 1000 and gradually displaced the Dorset.

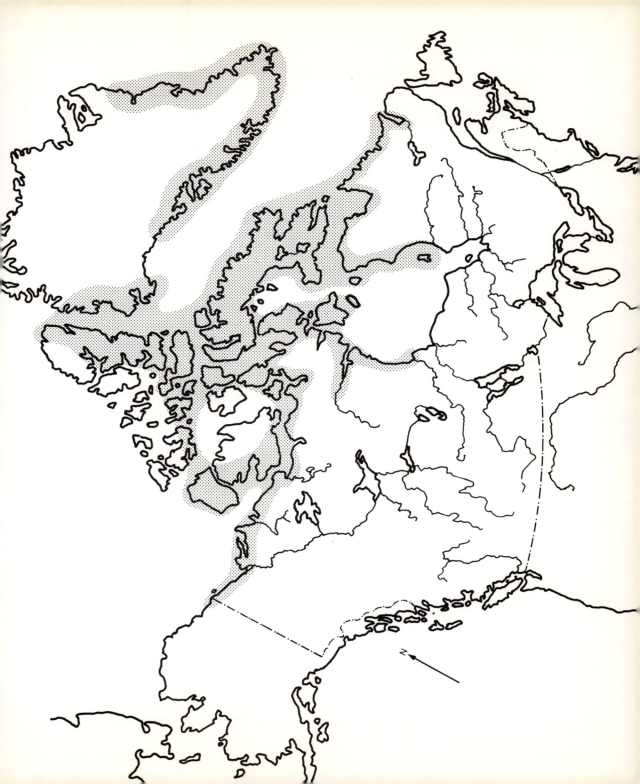

complexions. The women had blue streaks tattooed on their cheeks and around their eyes. Paintings by the artist John White, who accompanied the expedition in 1577, show clothes in styles the same as those observed in the early 1900s by Norwegian explorer Roald Amundsen. Having developed a practical set of garments for life in the Arctic, the people evidently saw no need to change.

The recorded accounts of these first encounters between the Inuit and the English paint a rather dismal picture of early race relations. The meetings were generally unfriendly. They were marked by fighting, killing, wounding and kidnapping. Frobisher himself was shot in the seat of the pants with an arrow! Inuit who were kidnapped and taken to England during Frobisher's first two voyages died of lung disease shortly after their stay began. Five English seamen kidnapped by Inuit were never seen again. An Inuit tradition later told of their drowning in a small boat in which they tried to sail away.

Several events besides the fighting and kidnapping occurred. These followed a pattern of events and developments which was repeated in other parts of the world in connection with early contacts between native peoples and incoming Europeans. The explorers carried ore back to the mother country in the expectation that it would produce gold and silver. Mining exploration thus became a major purpose of later voyages, including Frobisher's second and third expeditions. As was the case in both earlier and later European voyages of exploration, ceremonies were held claiming the land for the mother country. Monuments were raised to symbolize this takeover. During the Frobisher expeditions, as in many others, Europeans and natives seized each other's property as well as each other. Like the Indians taken to France by Cartier, the Inuit taken back to England by Frobisher were exhibited as curiosities until they died.

It proved to be impossible to refine gold or silver from the ore Frobisher took back to England. The apparent absence of precious metals in Inuit territory discouraged further contact on that basis. Hopes of finding the Northwest Passage died harder, however. Ten years later explorer John Davis led three more voyages to the Arctic. His encounters with the Inuit of Canada were similar to Frobisher's. By contrast, Davis's contacts with the Inuit of west-coast Greenland were better. At the old abandoned Viking settlement of Godthaab, Inuit traded fish, fowl and seal-skin clothes for European pins, needles, nails, bracelets, knives, belts and mirrors. They seem to have been especially eager to obtain metal objects. The English and the Inuit also joined in competitive games, dances, and musical entertainments. Clashes, kidnapping and killing also occurred, however.

These late sixteenth-century voyages mark the beginning of significant new contacts with Europeans. They also mark the end of the Thule era. The transformation of Thule culture into Inuit culture took place over several centuries. That slow transformation was by now virtually complete.

The True Inuit:
People of the Little Ice Age—
About 1600 to Late 1800s

The coming of the Thule was linked to the warming of temperatures sometime about A.D. 1000. The transformation of the Thule culture into a variety of cultures began to take place as early as the thirteenth century. It is associated with the cooling temperatures of the "Little Ice Age," which started about A.D. 1200 and reached its peak between 1600 and 1850. The native people of the North developed a variety of adjustments to these events and became the immediate forerunners of the modern Inuit.

During the "Little Ice Age," glaciers advanced. The tree line retreated southward. Animal distribution changed as the animals' food sources changed. Off the shores, the seas became shallower and choked with ice. The whales that had been so populous in the milder Thule period no longer came near enough to land for the Thule to hunt them. Ringed seal, caribou and musk-ox in particular now became key targets in the hunt.

Once again the adaptability of the northern people was tested. They responded, making changes in their way of life to suit natural changes.

The Inuit Way of Life
In the Inuit lifestyle, people could have few possessions, and these had to be portable. The young people learned to master necessary technology by watching and doing. Labour was divided by sex. Boys and girls learned their tasks in the family and community from male and female adults. Sharing was very important in a small community so exposed to the forces of nature. Starvation often threatened. Survival depended upon a delicate balance

Inuit children learned by watching and imitating their parents. By the time they were eight or nine they could do their share of the work. This boy has been cutting snow blocks to help build an igloo.

Inukshuk were made by piling large stones one on top of another into a shape roughly resembling a human being. Converging rows of them were used to channel caribou into confined areas where hunters waited, armed with bows and arrows. Inukshuk also sometimes served as guideposts to help travellers find their way across the featureless Arctic snows.

of skill, endurance and co-operation, aided by an ingenious technology. Tools, utensils and weapons were handmade by the user from the resources of bone, stone, ivory, wood, skins and other animal products—including feathers and claws. In the Mackenzie Valley area, iron could be added to the list, since this metal resource was discovered before European contact.

At certain times of the year, the people gathered in groups of a few hundred to hunt caribou or seals. But the basic Inuit community was small. It consisted of relatives, two or three families, under the leadership of a skilful hunter, an adult male. Everyone knew the affairs of everyone else. There were no secrets, and gossip was common. This situation called for tact and restraint, for self-control and a combination of tolerance of individual differences and sensitivity to the group's needs. Conflict had to be kept to a minimum. Differences that caused friction had to be settled within the group. Criticism or ridicule was the main form of social punishment. In extreme cases, a member might be expelled from the community, but this was dire punishment indeed. It meant almost certain death unless the exiled person could quickly find another group to join.

In so harsh an environment it was impossible to support many people who could make no contribution to the community. If circumstances were very bad and food so scarce that the survival of the group was threatened, the aged and the crippled might be left to die. Infants too were sometimes killed if they could not be cared for.

All across the Canadian Arctic, the Inuit shared a common language, Inuktitut. Regional variations developed, but these were relatively minor. The Inuit from all areas could understand one another.

Variety also developed in the design of clothing, but the same basic garments were worn by all Inuit: trousers and parkas made of skins, preferably caribou. All groups used kayaks, and many tools and utensils—such as soapstone lamps—were the same or similar in all areas. Large figures made of stacked stones, called Inuksuit or Inukshuk, were commonly used to guide travellers and drive caribou into ambush.

Spirit helpers, rituals and ceremonies aided in hunting and domestic tasks. Particularly careful attention was given to obtaining supernatural assistance for the hunt since the quest for food was so important and the supply was so often precarious. Shamans were employed for maintaining good relations with the supernatural and with the spirits of animals who gave their lives so that the people could live.

Periods of leisure were times for storytelling and entertainment. Until the nineteenth century, the Inuit did not have writing. Nonetheless, their stories and traditions constituted an oral "literature" that was preserved by the hearers and passed on by word of mouth. The oral literature of the Inuit told of the origins of things, of closeness between humans and animals and of the roles played by each in Inuit life. Stories telling of poor orphans who made good, of escapades, of raids and kidnapping, of individuals who possessed great strength were meant as more than entertainment. They demonstrated the importance of patience, calm, truthfulness, unselfishness. In other words, Inuit stories were the means by which new generations were taught the history and the morals and values of the people. Poetry, songs, stories and oratory were all closely linked in the oral literature of the Inuit.

Canadian Inuit Subgroups

There were nine Inuit subgroups distributed across northern Canada from Labrador to the Mackenzie Valley. Each group

Inuit stories were meant to educate as well as to entertain. Parents often illustrated their tales by making a succession of patterns with a long cord of sinew they wound around their fingers. The various patterns had symbolic meanings and represented animals, igloos and other familiar figures.

developed certain distinctive characteristics as a result of adaptation to local conditions and, in some cases, to contact with neighbouring Indian groups. Some Canadian Inuit groups had close cultural ties with Inuit of Greenland and Alaska Eskimos.

From east to west the Canadian groups were: the Labrador Inuit; the Ungava Inuit; the South Baffin Island Inuit; the Igloolik (Iglulik) Inuit, who occupied a large area including North Baffin Island and Foxe Basin; the Sadliq Inuit of Southampton Island; the Caribou Inuit of the west coast of Hudson Bay and the Barren Grounds; the Netsilik Inuit of the Central Arctic coast; the Copper Inuit, west of the Netsilik and mainly on Victoria Island; the Mackenzie Inuit of the Mackenzie delta area.[1]

Generally the Inuit lived along the coastlines and on the islands. Some areas, especially the interior of the major land masses, were largely unused because of limited food sources. Other areas, where food was more abundant, became centres of location. The people moved out from these centres to exploit nearby areas. The main exceptions to this pattern were the Caribou, or Barren Grounds Inuit. They lived primarily on the caribou in the interior west of Hudson Bay, and few ever even visited the coast. Other groups would move inland to hunt the caribou in summer. Caribou hides were important to all Inuit for clothing. Caribou sinew was used for sewing clothes and for making hunting gear. Caribou bones and antlers could be made into a variety of utensils, such as harpoons, arrowheads and thimbles.

The *Labrador Inuit* group was composed of over a dozen bands extending from the north shore of the Gulf of St. Lawrence to Ungava Bay. Although there was no tribal organization, each band was in contact with its neighbouring bands. Before the Europeans began coming regularly to this area, the people lived off a plentiful supply of walrus, caribou, whale and codfish. Codfish was not available to other Inuit groups.

Labrador Inuit enjoyed a rich variety of food, and thanks to

---

1 Diamond Jenness, one of Canada's greatest authorities on the Inuit, divided them into five cultural groups extending from east to west: the Labrador (including the Ungava), the Central, the Caribou, the Copper and the Mackenzie.

this plenty, they could live in large units. When the Europeans arrived, the Labrador Inuit were expanding southward along the east coast. Some crossed to Newfoundland, where they traded with the Beothuk Indians. A major trade item was hardwood for making bows and arrows. In their southward movement, the Labrador Inuit also met and competed with Algonkian-speaking Naskapi, Montagnais and Micmac Indians. At one time, the Labrador Inuit even occupied part of the north shore of the Gulf of St. Lawrence.

The *Ungava Inuit* of what is today northern Quebec resembled the Labrador Inuit, who were their eastern neighbours. The Ungava Inuit spoke the same dialect of Inuktitut and followed similar customs. Their ten bands hunted along the east coast of Hudson Bay as far south as the Eastmain River, and along the south coast of Hudson Strait and the west coast of Ungava Bay. In the summer, like other Inuit, Ungava Inuit bands went inland to hunt caribou and to fish. In general they avoided their interior neighbours, the Naskapi, though some contacts did occur.

The *South Baffin Island Inuit* were composed of seven bands. Each band was linked to its neighbours by marriage. Like the other groups, the South Baffin Island Inuit had no central organization or meeting place.

The way of life of the South Baffin Island people closely resembled that of their neighbours, the *Igloolik Inuit*. The Igloolik occupied a large area including North Baffin Island. Scholars often treat the Igloolik, the South Baffin Island people and the Netsilik as one group, calling them the Central Inuit. The Igloolik hunted walrus and baleen whale. They kept large numbers of dogs, which they fed from the abundant meat supplies available to them. In housebuilding, they used whale bones, stone and turf. The plentiful food supply of the Igloolik contributed to a material culture richer than that of their neighbours.

The *Sadliq Inuit* of Southampton Island are less well-known than other groups. Like the Igloolik, they built with stone, whale

Map showing the location of the nine Inuit sub-groups.

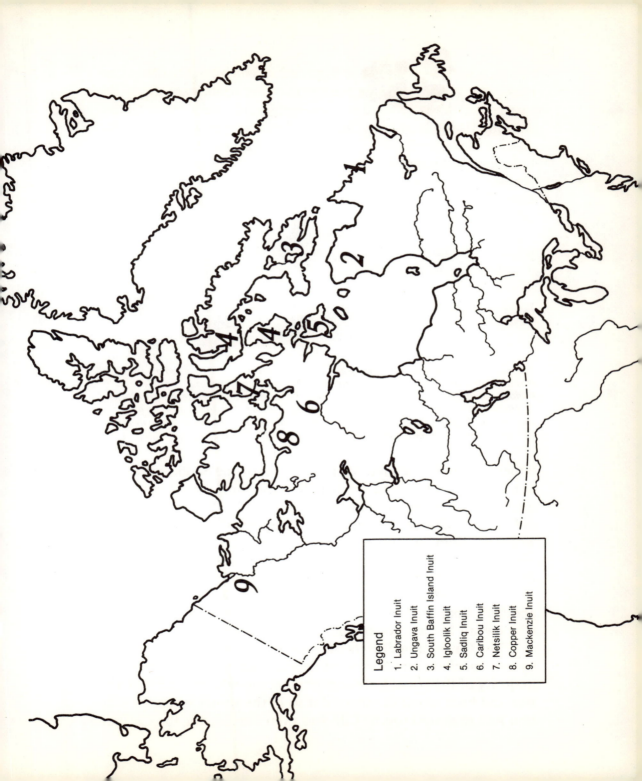

Legend
1. Labrador Inuit
2. Ungava Inuit
3. South Baffin Island Inuit
4. Igloolik Inuit
5. Sadliq Inuit
6. Caribou Inuit
7. Netsilik Inuit
8. Copper Inuit
9. Mackenzie Inuit

The domed snow house, or igloo, was the winter home of most Canadian Inuit. It was also used by all groups as a temporary shelter when travelling. A skilled builder could put one up in an hour or two. Using a long flat knife he cut blocks of packed snow which he placed one on top of another in a spiral around him, each block sloping inward a little. He chinked the cracks with loose snow to make the igloo windproof and sometimes added a piece of clear lake ice as a window.

bones and turf. The material possessions of the Sadliq have been described as cruder and simpler than those of other Inuit. They used bearskins for clothing more commonly than other groups did, and unlike other Inuit, they frequently used flint-headed weapons. Some writers think the Sadliq may have been Dorset survivors or had some Dorset as well as Thule elements. In 1902, the Sadliq died out due to an epidemic of typhus.

The *Caribou Inuit* mentioned earlier were composed of about five bands. In the eighteenth century they fought with the Chipewyan Indians for the use of hunting grounds.

The Caribou Inuit were the most different from other groups by reason of their almost total dependence on the caribou. The majority of them had little or nothing to do with the sea. The few who did hunt along the shore did so in the winter when the caribou had migrated south. Life was even harsher for the Caribou

Inuit than for most other groups. They used caribou fat for lamp oil the same way the coastal Inuit used blubber, but it was less efficient as a fuel, providing light but little warmth. Survival through the winter depended on a surplus of caribou being taken and cached in the fall. If anything interfered with the fall hunt, the Caribou Inuit had virtually no alternative food sources to turn to in the winter. As a result they suffered more than most other Inuit groups from food shortages and starvation.

The *Netsilik Inuit* lived in seven small bands on or near King William Island. They are particularly associated with seal hunting, which they pursued through much of the year. The Netsilik were in infrequent contact with their Dene Indian neighbours to the south.

The Netsilik's Inuit neighbours to the west were the *Copper Inuit* of Victoria Island, named for the copper found on the island. The Copper Inuit were divided into six or seven bands. Sealing was a major part of their life.

Across the north, the Inuit hunted seal at their breathing holes, but the Copper Inuit were especially expert at this form of sealing. Since there was no way of controlling when the seal would come to a particular hole, this kind of hunting required the utmost patience. Hunters had to wait, perfectly still, for hours and hours despite cold, hunger, isolation and uncertainty about successfully taking the seal when it did appear. In the summer the Copper Inuit fished and hunted on the land, mainly musk-ox and caribou. Like some other western groups, the Copper Inuit had occasional contact with the Dene Indians.

The *Mackenzie Inuit* most resembled the Alaskan Eskimos. They occupied the Mackenzie River delta and consisted of five main bands. In the summer they sometimes gathered in camps of as many as a thousand people to hunt whale. In a good summer they might take up to two hundred whales. A catch of such size could easily support them for the year. Elements of Mackenzie Inuit clothing and equipment differed in some aspects from those of the more easterly Inuit peoples. Mackenzie Inuit sometimes traded and fought with neighbouring Dene peoples, the Hare and Kutchin.

Europeans Bring Change

As we have seen, internal changes—primarily climatic—and adaptation to these changes led to regional groupings. The relatively uniform Thule culture was replaced by more varied Inuit local cultures. At the same time, new influences that caused other changes were beginning to be introduced from outside.

By the seventeenth century, contacts and trade were occurring fairly frequently between the Inuit and European explorers, whalers and fur traders. The Inuit traded animal pelts, food and knowledge of the land and waters. Some occasionally worked on European ships. In return for their goods and expertise, they wanted European manufactured goods, especially, at least at first, metal tools.

It was not only direct contact with Europeans that affected the Inuit. By the seventeenth and eighteenth centuries, neighbouring Indian peoples had acquired guns and were pressing against the Inuit. To resist and counter these pressures, the Inuit too wished to get European firearms.

In general, the Indians recognized the land beyond the tree line as Inuit territory and did not occupy it or even, in most cases, try to use it. But before the Indians acquired European firearms, the Inuit occupied much more territory than they do today. Armed Montagnais and Micmac Indians pushed them out of the Gulf of St. Lawrence area and, with European help, beyond the Strait of Belle Isle. Cree with guns forced the Inuit northward from the Eastmain River to the Great Whale River. The Caribou Inuit at one time hunted as far south as Churchill. Once the Chipewyans had guns, they banished the Inuit from the Churchill area to Eskimo Point. Eventually conflict between Indian and Inuit occurred in the western Arctic as well, particularly in the area of Fort McPherson, a Hudson's Bay Company trading post established in the mid-nineteenth century.

Explorers, Whalers and Fur Traders

By the late eighteenth century, whalers were hunting regularly in the waters between Greenland and Baffin Island. Explorers were still seeking the Northwest Passage as well as new sources of pelts

In the past, an Inuit family used a raised sleeping and seating platform of their igloo. The platform, like the igloo itself, was made of snow. Some of the skins that served as tent coverings in summer were spread over it to keep the people warmer and to prevent their body heat from melting the snow.

for the fur trade companies that employed them. Henry Hudson had visited the Ungava Peninsula in the early seventeenth century, and by mid-eighteenth century the Hudson's Bay Company was carrying out operations in the territory of the Ungava Inuit. In 1771 Samuel Hearne, a Hudson's Bay Company trader, penetrated westward to the Coppermine River. In 1789, Alexander Mackenzie explored the river that today bears his name.

In the early and mid-nineteenth century, explorers continued to penetrate the territories of the Inuit. George Back, John Ross and John Rae visited the Netsilik. George Lyon and William Parry explored the Central Arctic and met and described the Igloolik. John Rae also visited the Igloolik and George Lyon, in the course of his exploration, visited the Sadliq Inuit of Southampton Island.

In the summer, all groups of Inuit lived in tupeks—*tents made of seal or caribou skins. The edges of the tent were held down with rocks which were left behind when the people moved on. Although this picture was taken many years ago, the circle of rocks probably still identifies the spot where this tupek stood.*

John Franklin and others visited the Mackenzie Inuit. In 1848 the people of the Mackenzie delta were again visited by John Richardson during his search for Franklin, who had mysteriously disappeared on a journey of exploration. Explorers and others who contacted the Inuit often hired them as guides, interpreters and labourers.

Whalers had at least occasionally visited the waters off Greenland and Labrador as early as the sixteenth century. But it was in the early 1700s that the great eastern Arctic whale fisheries really began. Scottish whalers in particular exploited this area. In the beginning, encounters between the Inuit and Europeans were not regular or routine. In time, however, contact became more regular. Some European whalers began wintering in the North. The Inuit tended to welcome them for the trade goods they offered.

Inuit men worked for the whalers as hunters, pilots, boat crews, food suppliers and harpooners. Inuit women sewed clothing and gear. Payment was always made in goods and supplies, not in money. Sometimes fights occurred when whalers poached on Inuit hunting areas, or kidnapped Inuit women. Gradually the Inuit were learning about and selecting for their own use elements of European culture, especially tools, weapons and materials that could be fitted into their ways of living.

Unfortunately, European diseases and other problems were also being introduced. By the late nineteenth century there was widespread population decline among the Inuit because of their lack of natural resistance to diseases such as smallpox, tuberculosis, scarlet fever and measles. Among the goods supplied by the Europeans was alcohol, or the means to make it (molasses and potatoes). Excessive use of alcohol led to violence resulting in injuries and death. Conflicts between Europeans and Inuit occurred when cheating and stealing happened, or were thought to be happening. The whalers also brought in venereal diseases.

By the middle and late nineteenth century, western Arctic waters were being regularly visited by American whalers who came from San Francisco by way of the Bering Sea. Whalebone (as baleen is commonly and somewhat confusingly called) was

The Inuit used a number of fishing techniques, from jigging through a hole in the ice with line made of braided sinew to spearing larger fish from rocks above the water. Here Copper Inuit in the Coronation Gulf area have built stone weirs across shallow water to trap salmon trout swimming upstream. Small openings allow the fish through the lower rows and a closed dam farther upstream prevents them from escaping. The fishermen can then spear them easily with their long-handled three-pronged leisters.

highly prized. Because of its lightness and flexibility, it was in great demand for use in women's corsets, and the whalebone from one bowhead whale could be worth up to $10,000. Whale oil was also in demand. Other whale products were used in perfume making. Whalers hired Inuit to supply caribou meat and to gather driftwood for fuel. Inuit assistants were especially useful when whalers began to winter in the North, and the whalers transported them from one location to another to suit their needs.

By the late nineteenth and early twentieth century, the number of whales had been greatly reduced, first in the eastern Arctic and then in the West. Gradually the whaling ships stopped coming. But by this time, the Inuit had become dependent on European goods and supplies. Their requirements would now have to be met from other European sources. These sources were to be the fur trader and the missionary. Just about the time whaling began to decline and the Inuit needed an alternative way of obtaining European trade goods, the demand for furs in Europe and North America greatly expanded. Furs were now no longer only the fashion of the wealthy.

Missionaries Among the Inuit

Christian missionaries began to reach most of the Inuit in the late nineteenth century. The two main demoninations were the Roman Catholic and the Anglican. But almost a hundred years before either of these set up regular missions in the Arctic, the Moravian Brethren had established themselves among the Labrador Inuit of the Atlantic coast. The Labrador coast was

To preserve fish after a good summer catch, the Inuit cut it up and spread it out in the sun on rocks and lines to dry.

then under the authority of British colonial administrators in St. John's, Newfoundland (Newfoundland was not yet part of Canada), but it was largely ignored by government. When the Moravian Brethen came into the area, they established mission stations along the whole eight-hundred-kilometre stretch from Hamilton Inlet to Cape Chidley.

In 1765, Jens Haven, a Moravian Brethren missionary in Greenland, met Inuit from Hamilton Inlet. Through his efforts, contact was established between the Labrador Inuit and the British governor of Newfoundland, and peace was restored along the coast, which had previously been troubled by clashes between Inuit and European traders. From this contact the mission at Nain was begun in 1771, and other missions followed.

A mission consisted of a dwelling for the missionary and his family, a church, a trading store (the missionary doubled as a trader) and a workshop. Labrador Inuit soon began to build their winter homes at the mission sites, and villages grew up. As well as evangelists bringing the Christian Gospel, the Moravian missionaries became the unofficial agents of government and of European culture.

Most Moravian missionaries were from Germany, but they learned to live close to the Inuit. They mastered the Inuit language and preached in Inuktitut. The close Moravian–Inuit relationship continued well into the twentieth century. As the Inuit settled into the Moravian communities it became unnecessary for them to trade with others who might hunt or hurt them, or who might introduce influences thought to be undesirable by the missionaries. As far as the outside world was concerned, the Labrador Inuit were largely ignored and the area was not of great interest until the second half of the nineteenth century.

Between 1850 and 1900, a number of Newfoundland fishermen came to the coast, and fishing settlements were established south of the Moravian–Inuit villages. Racially mixed commun-

---

On sunny spring days, the Inuit wore snow goggles made of driftwood or ivory to protect their eyes. The narrow slits cut down the glare of the sun reflecting on the snow without significantly limiting the field of vision.

INUKTITUT ᐃᓄᒃ ᑎᑐᑦ

△ i	▷ u	◁ a			
∧ pi	> pu	> pa	‹		
∩ ti	⊃ tu	⊂ ta	ៅ		
ᑭ ki	ᑯ ku	ᑲ ka	ᑉ		
ᒋ gi	ᒍ gu	ᒐ ga	ᒡ		
ᒥ mi	ᒧ mu	ᒪ ma	ᒻ		
σ ni	ᓄ nu	ᓇ na	ᓐ	H ·	
ᓯ si / hi	ᓱ su / hu	ᓴ sa / ha	ᔅ	·	
ᒡ li	ᓗ lu	ᓚ la	ᓪ	ᔨ	
ᔨ ji	ᔪ ju	ᔭ ja	ᔾ		
ᕕ vi	ᕗ vu	ᕙ va	ᕝ		
ᕆ ri	ᕈ ru	ᕋ ra	ᕐ		
ᕿ qi	ᖁ qu	ᖃ qa	ᖅ		
ᖨ &i	ᖑ &u	ᖓ &a	ᖕ		
ᖏ ngi	ᖐ ngu	ᖓ nga	ᐟ		

This system for writing Inuktitut is called a syllabary because the characters represent syllables. It was devised by the Reverend E. J. Peck, who adapted the Cree syllabary developed by the Reverend James Evans, a Methodist missionary.

ities developed under the spiritual, educational and social direction of the missionaries. Then the Hudson's Bay Company began to take an interest in the area. In 1925 the Moravian Brethren leased their trading rights, stores and wharves to the Hudson's Bay Company for twenty-one years.

The Moravian communities were generally peaceful. Literacy was 90 percent, crime was almost unknown and there were no police or jails. In 1934 the government of Newfoundland assumed authority over Labrador and sent police to the area. The church withdrew from its political and social services role. Further changes followed with the introduction of motor boats and later airplanes. Like the rest of the Inuit, the Labrador Inuit experienced an upsurge in the fur trade. Seal hunting and cod fishing declined. A greater dependency on the outside world resulted. As in other areas, the increase in commercial hunting led to the rapid destruction of wildlife.

The first missionary to the western Arctic was Father Emile Petitot of the Oblates of Mary Immaculate. The Oblate fathers were organized in early nineteenth-century France and came to Canada about the middle of the century. They became the main missionary order of the Roman Catholic Church in western and northern Canada. Father Petitot visited the Mackenzie Inuit briefly in 1868 and compiled a grammar of their language. In 1872 Father Charles Renaud, also an Oblate, pioneered Roman Catholic missions in the eastern Arctic when he began a mission at Fort Chimo. Major expansion occurred in the twentieth century.

Anglican presence in the eastern Arctic was established by the Reverend E. J. Peck, who set up several missions between 1876 and 1894. On one occasion, Peck had the experience of building a church out of materials similar to those used in Inuit architecture. The framework was of whale bones and the covering of sealskin. Unfortunately the church was later eaten by hungry dogs!

In 1876 Peck adapted the Cree syllabary invented by the Methodist missionary James Evans to the language of the Inuit. He used parts of the New Testament translated by Moravian

Brethren missionaries of Labrador. In 1894 he took his system of writing to Baffin Island. Reading spread rapidly among the northern native people as Inuit taught other Inuit in areas where no Europeans had been.

In the western Arctic, Anglican missions were pioneered by the Reverend, later Bishop, Isaac O. Stringer. His travels and brushes with starvation caused him to be known as the "bishop who ate his boots."

Rivalry among the three churches—Anglican, Moravian Brethren and Roman Catholic—which dominated mission work among the Inuit was generally avoided by agreements to respect one another's areas of membership.

Thule–Inuit History— A Story of Change and Adaptation

From the late eighteenth century down to the early twentieth century, the Inuit traditional life continued but was modified by European contact, trade goods, population movement, racial mixing and disease. These elements were introduced by explorers, whalers, fur traders and missionaries. The Inuit were faced with all of these changes at a time when they were still evolving from the previous Thule culture for reasons not related to the arrival of the Europeans.

Thus, the incoming Europeans saw the Inuit not as they had been from some earlier time, but in a new adaptation that they were in the process of developing. This adaptation, as we have seen, was prompted by climate changes and their effects on flora and fauna.

Inuit and the Outsiders Who Came to Stay—Late 1800s to Mid-1900s

Up to the period of the Europeans and their written records, historians have to reconstruct Inuit history from oral tradition and archaeology. As a result, little attention is given the contribution of individuals in early Inuit history. The politicians, diplomats, military leaders, religious leaders, financial wizards, saints and sinners who are the subject matter of so much history are missing from much of the story of the Inuit until quite recently. Europeans often described the Inuit as being without government, society or religion. This is not completely true. But the organization of the society was so different from that of European or southern Canadian society that it is difficult to describe it in the usual terms of "state," "class," "church," "labour," and so on. The way of life of the Inuit thus becomes the main subject matter of early Inuit history.

A different problem arises in the writing of more recent Inuit history. It was the Europeans who kept the written records from which history is usually reconstructed. Inuit individuals who are known to us are therefore those who had the closest contact with the Europeans. The facts, events and developments recorded are those which the Europeans witnessed or heard of. One result of this situation is that Inuit history becomes to a large extent the story of Inuit–white contact and of the effects and changes, conflicts and co-operation, that this contact produced.

The Inuit in the Fur Trade Era
In the early twentieth century, the Inuit found themselves hosts to

traders and missionaries. The people still lived by hunting, trapping and fishing, but they now used mainly weapons and tools introduced from outside. The dependence begun in the commercial whaling era continued into the new fur trade era. The coming of the fur traders intensified the search for fur-bearing animals. The intensified hunting coupled with the ease of killing with guns led to the rapid destruction of wildlife. The pattern established with the whalers was thus repeated. As we have seen, the extension of hunting into the territory of other Inuit or of Indians sometimes led to conflict.

A few trading posts had been built in or near Inuit territory in the eighteenth and nineteenth centuries, but the major expansion took place in the first three decades of the twentieth century. Trading posts began to spring up in most regions, and the Inuit began to visit them regularly. Individual bands attached themselves to particular posts. The Hudson's Bay Company was the main trading agent but individual traders and other companies, including Révillon Frères, a firm based in Paris, France, also operated posts. Some whalers turned to fur trading, and some Inuit became traders.

A visitor to Cumberland Sound, Baffin Island, described a typical trading scene there in 1903. In January and February the people came to the post and stayed for several days preparing the pelts to be traded. No cash was used in the transaction. Instead, tokens were given representing the value of the pelts in terms of white fox skins. The white fox was the standard of the Inuit fur trade just as the beaver was the standard for so long in the Indian fur trade. A blue fox was equivalent to two white fox skins. A silver fox was equivalent to between fifteen and forty white fox skins, and so on, with various differing values for otter, marten, mink, white bear and deer. Each had its equivalence. The Inuit hunters used the tokens they received to purchase tobacco, ammunition, tin kettles, knives, files and whatever else they needed, until all their tokens were spent.

A trapper poses proudly with his catch of white fox pelts.

Besides hunting and trapping, Inuit were employed by the traders as guides, interpreters, carvers, sled drivers, maintenance workers, harpooners and gardeners. During the long period of contact with explorers and whalers the Inuit had discovered that the Europeans liked to take home their carvings of bone, ivory and wood as souvenirs. They now began to make more of these carvings, mainly figures of animals and humans, specifically for trading purposes.

Increasingly, the Inuit relied for subsistence not just on what they could acquire with the old technology or from use of the new, but on what they could buy at a trader's store. They paid for what they bought at the store, with the pelts of animals they hunted and trapped with equipment also bought at the store.

As more goods were introduced by the traders, the dependence of the Inuit increased. By the early decades of the twentieth century, the kayak and umiak were largely replaced by imported manufactured boats. Guns had changed hunting techniques. No longer did the Inuit drive the caribou or chase them into the water in order to kill them more easily. Ambushes and snares were made unnecessary by the use of the rifle. Canvas tents replaced skin tents. English words and even English grammar were creeping into the everyday language of the Inuit. More racial mixing was taking place. High prices for furs in the early decades allowed some Inuit to earn large amounts of money. They could thus afford large boats which they used for travelling to hunting grounds, carrying freight and visiting with friends and neighbours.

The fur traders adapted to the Inuit to a greater degree than the whalers or explorers had. The earlier Europeans may have suffered unduly because of their failure to adapt, especially in matters of clothing and food. Traders, by contrast, were not there just on short visits as most of the whalers and explorers had been. They realized that their livelihood was closely tied to the land and its people. Sometimes they intermarried with the Inuit.

The fur trade era not only increased Inuit contact with whites, it also led to greater contact between Inuit and Indian. In the East, the Inuit's main neighbouring Indian peoples are the

Hunting walrus on ice floes can be dangerous. A shift in wind can cause channels of open water to widen and strand the hunters on the drifting ice. Here a hunter urges his dogs across a widening crack. He will follow by using a long sled as a bridge.

eastern sub-Arctic Algonkian speakers, such as the Naskapi, Montagnais and Cree. In the West, their major Indian neighbours are the sub-Arctic Athapaskan speakers (Dene), such as the Chipewyan, Hare and Loucheux. Inuit and Indian peoples met at trading posts and were sometimes rivals for the hunting and trapping use of the land.

The fur trade boom came to an end in the 1930s when a great worldwide depression occurred. The Inuit, tied as they now were to the commercial economy of the outside world, were hard hit by the sharp decline of the world market for their pelts. No longer could furs be relied on as a major source of income. But the Inuit were now dependent on weapons, ammunition, tools, clothes and food that had to be bought. Many suffered a great deal as they tried to find new ways to purchase these necessities from the shrinking number of trading posts. In the 1940s fox prices began to rise again, but by that time World War II was bringing new and different opportunities for Inuit employment.

Disease, Declining Population and Medical Help

The Inuit population had declined in the 1800s as a result of epidemic diseases introduced by the whalers. Increased contact with whites contributed to a further decline of population that continued into the early decades of the twentieth century. The Inuit had no natural immunities to European diseases, and neither their shamans' healing techniques nor the medical knowledge of the newcomers could prevent great losses of life. In 1842 an influenza epidemic struck the Labrador Inuit, and in 1876 they were subject to a spread of whooping cough. The Inuit in the vicinity of Anderson River were victims of a scarlet fever outbreak in 1865. In the same year, influenza reduced the Copper Inuit by one-third. The Mackenzie Inuit were struck by measles in 1902. Two-thirds of the Inuit in some regions of Labrador died in the 1918 influenza epidemic. Ten years later large numbers of the

The crossboards of the Inuit dogsled, or komatik, *were lashed to the runners with sinew. The runners were coated with mud and then sprayed with water to form a thin film of ice that made them slide more easily across the snow. The size of the komatik varied. Some were over five metres long, and as many as twelve dogs might be hitched to such a large sled.*

Herschel Island people contracted the same disease. (The survivors of the Herschel Island outbreak moved to Tuktoyaktuk.) Epidemics are estimated to have killed more than ninety percent of the Inuit population in some communities. Only one woman and four children, for instance, survived the epidemic that destroyed the Sadliq Inuit in 1902. They were removed to the mainland, where only two children were still alive in 1907. Beyond that date there is no record of them.

The first doctor to visit the Inuit regularly was Wilfred Grenfell. His main work was with the fishing fleet, but in 1892 he began making calls each summer along the Labrador coast. In about 1898 the Moravians established a hospital at Hopedale headed by a member of their clergy who was trained in medicine. A hospital and medical doctor operated at Okak, Labrador between 1902 and 1908. Some observers thought that the shift from the traditional Inuit diet of fresh or sun-dried meat and fish had weakened the people. Others reported that only the very high birth rate of the Inuit prevented their total extinction under the onslaught of the high death rate. By 1930 the western Arctic population was placed at about two hundred, down from an estimated two thousand in the 1830s.

In areas of Inuit territory other than Labrador, missions and the government began to build hospitals in the 1920s. Gradually the population stabilized and began to increase. The conquest of diseases was not complete, however, even by the mid-twentieth century. In 1950 it was estimated that 20 percent of all Inuit were suffering from tuberculosis. Canada's Inuit population in 1939 was approximately seven thousand, not including Labrador. By 1958 Labrador was part of Canada, and the estimated Inuit population for Canada was almost nine thousand.

New Contacts, New Settlements, New Ideas
In the first half of the twentieth century, the Mackenzie Inuit came into frequent and intensive contact with the Alaska Eskimos. The cultures of the two peoples mingled, and strong resemblances developed between them. Whites coming in from Alaska also intermixed with the Mackenzie Inuit.

62

The people of the Mackenzie delta were less hard hit by the collapse in fur prices than other Inuit because they were not as closely tied to the fur trade as other groups. In the 1940s they trapped muskrats and enjoyed a period of good prices for the pelts. This prosperity caused neighbouring Alaskan Inuit, Indians and whites to come into the Mackenize area to trap. Rivalry among trappers soon led to disputes, and in 1948 the government introduced the registration of traplines in order to put an end to conflicting claims.

Some whaling continued in Cumberland Sound, in southeast Baffin Island and on the coast of Labrador. In the nineteenth century whalers had a station at Kekerten Island, near the mouth of the Pangnirtung fiord. In 1921 the Hudson's Bay Company built a port at the fiord, and the settlement of Pangnirtung began. Two years later a police post was established, and four years after that the Anglican Church mission built a hospital. Pangnirtung was one of several new settlements that were beginning to be established. Such settlements usually grew up around installations created by the whites, whether whalers, missionaries, police or fur traders. The location was chosen to suit the purpose of the installation.

We see the same pattern in the settlement of Coppermine at the mouth of the Coppermine River. In 1927 a Hudson's Bay Company post was erected. Two years later Anglican and Roman Catholic missions were established nearby. In the following two years a government hospital was built. Similarly Cambridge Bay, in the southeastern Victoria Island, grew up around a Hudson's Bay Company trading post established in 1923, then closed in 1925 and reopened two years later.

Among a number of other communities that came into existence in the first three decades of this century were Aklavik, Cape Dorset, Frobisher Bay and Tuktoyaktuk.

In order to give greater economic stability and variety to the Inuit economy, some interesting but unsuccessful experiments were tried.

A herd of reindeer was introduced among the Labrador Inuit in the early 1900s. Reindeer have been an important part of the

Inuit hunters were once expert archers, but few use a bow and arrow today. Rifles are much more efficient. This has, in the not-so-far-distant past, meant misery and starvation for some, particularly among the Caribou Inuit. Herds were depleted, and sometimes even if a few animals appeared the hunters could not kill them. Trading posts within reach had closed down, they could not buy ammunition for their rifles, and the old skills with bow and arrow had been lost.

economy of the Lapp, or Sami, people of northern Scandinavia, who take their food and clothing from these useful animals. In 1913 the Labrador herd numbered about fifteen hundred, but it declined to about two hundred and thirty by 1916 as a result of poaching. The remnant of the herd was later removed to Anticosti Island and died there.

At about this time (1914-1918), the explorer Vilhjalmur Stefansson was travelling in the western half of the Arctic archipelago. In his report he suggested that reindeer be introduced there. The Hudson's Bay Company accordingly brought in over six hundred reindeer from Norway. The natural foods necessary for their survival were not available in that area, however, and

This woman is playing a favourite Inuit game, trying to catch a piece of wood with holes in it on a peg. Sometimes the skull of a hare or other small animal was used instead of the piece of wood. Notice the tattoo marks on the woman's face and arms. Tattooing was done by passing a needle threaded with soot-covered sinew under the skin or by pricking the skin with a needle dipped in a mixture of grease and soot. The practice was abandoned in the early twentieth century.

many died or were dispersed. The remainder were returned to Norway.

The idea of creating reindeer herds in the Canadian North was again proposed in 1922, this time by a federal government Royal Commission. Although some non-Inuit experts were doubtful, herds were brought in the 1920s and early 1930s, and Laplanders were hired as technical advisers in their care. This experiment too was a failure.

Another course of action taken to change economic conditions was government assistance in relocating Inuit from impoverished areas to ones richer in resources or to a depopulated area. One example was the removal of people from Baffin Island to Devon Island. A side effect of this action was to help establish Canada's claim in the far northern islands.

Missionary Activity and Influence

Missionary posts continued to expand in the twentieth century. Their presence intensified the impact of outside influences. Missionaries acted as doctors, dentists, engineers, traders, teachers and in a variety of other capacities. Like the traders, the missionaries were also employers. Inuit worked for them in construction, maintenance, guiding and interpreting. Inuit were key figures in the work and survival of early missionaries. In 1870 a man called Shaputartuk acted as guide to a well-known Anglican missionary, the Reverend William C. Bompas of the Church Missionary Society (CMS). Years later his son, Takatshimak, guided another CMS missionary, the Reverend I. O. Stringer. Later some Inuit became clergymen, for example the Reverend Thomas Mook, who worked with Stringer and was ordained in 1926.

Missionaries and traders sometimes came into conflict with each other over their dealings with the people. Missionaries opposed the use of alcohol in trading. They also favoured keeping Sunday as a day of worship and rest and sought to prevent disruption of family life. The loss of time from hunting meant fewer pelts for the traders.

For a long time the Inuit culture retained its character and vigour as the people were able to absorb the changes introduced gradually. In those circumstances missionaries were accepted according to their ability to make a contribution to the existing culture. Their teachings and ideas were strange, of course, and they met with some opposition, particularly from Inuit shamans who felt that their position as religious leaders and controllers of the supernatural was being threatened. Many shamans, however, like other Inuit, simply absorbed Christian teachings into their own traditions.

The missionaries exerted many positive, practical influences on Inuit community life. They helped reduce violence and abuses associated with alcohol. They gave medical help and served as go-betweens in Inuit relations with other whites. They sometimes learned the language, and this increased their ability to act as interpreters of Inuit ways. While to some degree they contributed to the disruption and destruction of some elements of Inuit culture, they also played a role in preserving others. In particular, they helped safeguard the Inuit language by developing a writing system for Inuktitut.

Some Inuit developed their own forms of Inuit Christianity. Others, taught by missionaries or influenced by Christianity, sought to mix the old beliefs and customs with the new religion and produce a new religious blend. At Igloolik in 1921, Umik led an effort to create an Inuit Christian group. In 1969 the first Inuit Anglican priest in the eastern Arctic, the Reverend Armand Togoonak, left the Anglican church to start an Inuit Christian church. Inuit acting as lay preachers and missionaries spread Christianity to Inuit who were not in contact with missionaries from outside. In recent years the churches have become strong defenders of the land rights and other claims of the Inuit.

The RCMP, Representatives of Canadian Government

For several decades the Inuit were in contact with the Canadian government primarily through the presence of the North West Mounted Police (renamed the Royal Canadian Mounted Police after World War I).

In 1880 Canada received title to the Arctic islands, but not until 1897 was a ship sent to proclaim Canada's legal authority over Baffin Island and other islands north of the mainland. During the next few years, a Norwegian expedition of exploration seemed to threaten Canada's claim. In 1903 the first North West Mounted Police were sent to establish a post at Fullerton Harbour, a wintering station for whaling vessels on the northwest coast of Hudson Bay. A second police post was created at Port Burwell on the south shore of Hudson Strait. Documents were deposited at several places proclaiming Canada's sovereignty in the northern islands, including Ellesmere Island where the Norwegians had established their base. In the same year, 1903, the first two police posts were created in the western Arctic at Fort

McPherson and on Herschel Island. The former was a Hudson's Bay Company trading post, and the latter was a wintering station for American whalers. The police had authority to inspect ships' cargoes, collect taxes and duties, confiscate liqour and keep the peace.

Such government actions, while establishing Canada's rights to the northern islands in terms of international law and custom, had little or nothing to do with accepting responsibility for the Inuit. In 1905 a commissioner for the Northwest Territories was created, but the main purpose of this office was maintaining law and order through the police stationed in the North. Nonetheless, like the missionaries, the police often found themselves involved with the Inuit in other capacities. Insofar as any agency could be said to be "in charge" of Inuit, it was the police under the commissioner of Northwest Territories.

The long, dark days of winter were a time for socializing, for getting together to play games, sing, dance and talk. Here a group of Copper Inuit watch and chant as one member dances while whirling and beating a skin drum.

Through the 1920s more police stations and police patrols were added. A patrol ship was sent to the northern waters. In 1924 the Inuit were placed under the Department of Indian Affairs for administrative purposes. (That department had actually given aid to the Inuit in the Mackenzie delta as far back as 1880.) The Inuit, however, did not have the same status as Indians. They were not wards under the Indian Act (1876), and they had no treaties or land surrenders.

Government activity in the North had meanwhile been increasing. As we have seen, the government had made efforts in connection with creating reindeer herds, relocating people and expanding police services. In 1939 the expenditure on Inuit amounted to over $200,000, more than half of which was spent on police.

The Inuit on the Eve of World War II

The Second World War and postwar periods were to see drastic changes in the life of the northern native peoples. The first half of the twentieth century had witnessed the increasing control of Inuit economic, religious and legal life by traders, missionaries and police. The Inuit continued to control their day-to-day decisions, and most communities were largely native in population. Sometimes they were of Inuit and Indian composition, as at Fort Chimo where both Inuit and Naskapi lived. Family and kinship ties continued. Hunting, trapping and meat-sharing took place within the family or kinship group. Traditional controls still regulated group life despite the presence of the Mounties. Native spiritual life existed alongside the Christianity introduced by missionaries. It was an era of cultural contact and technological change. But Inuit life was still rooted in Inuit culture.

Contentemporary Concerns

World War II opened up new economic opportunities for the Inuit. It brought a great expansion of construction in the North—roads, bridges, wharves, airports, airfields, hangars, houses, barracks, office buildings, maintenance facilities, mining installations, and so on. The Inuit were drawn into the boom. Handicrafts and fishing found expanded markets. Even more significantly, there was an increased need for people to carry, load, lift, haul and do maintenance work. Jobs as unskilled and semi-skilled labourers took the place of those in the fur trade, just as those in the fur trade had previously replaced employment in whaling. Although they were not the best jobs, they brought a new prosperity to the Inuit. But this prosperity did not last long. The flurry of activity ended with the war and so did the jobs it had provided.

In the 1950s, the "Cold War" between the United States and the Soviet Union renewed the boom of the war years. Inuit life was being affected more and more by events occurring far from the Canadian North. Listening posts to detect aircraft were installed across the Arctic. The erection and maintenance of the "Distance Early Warning" (DEW) line created another brief era of jobs, again mostly unskilled and semi-skilled as far as Inuit were concerned.

During both World War II and the Cold War periods, there was a great influx of Canadian and American military and technical personnel. Surveys, research and mapping increased. Airfields were built in small villages to aid travel and communication. Diamond Jenness, an expert on Canadian Inuit administration, said of this period,

The Second World War, and the Cold War which succeeded it, convulsed Canada's far north as it did Labrador and Greenland. It bared to the world the ineptitude of her administration and the degradation of her Eskimos, many of whom it dragged out of their isolation and caught up in its turmoil.

Postwar Developments

In the postwar era the Inuit began to see more activity by the federal government. The fur trader, missionary and police declined in relative importance as furs became less important to the economy. Government took over schools, hospitals and other social services that had previously been performed by missionaries. A variety of governmental personnel now began to deal with the Inuit. By the end of the 1970s, Inuit themselves were part of the local and territorial governments.

Inuit communities underwent changes. These communities, which were relatively recent in origin, lacked economic stability and self-sufficiency. They lacked the internal unity characteristic of earlier villages composed of one band, or of related groups. Outside influences were stronger, deeper and more widespread than ever before. Many "modern" communities of the North had been created by the war and the postwar needs of the whites. Prior to the coming of whites, the main feature of relations between Inuit and Indians had always been either conflict or avoidance of each other. Now—in mixed communities of Inuit, Indians and whites—the Inuit and Indians were actually present because of the whites.

These newer mixed communities have shown signs of developing class or even caste-like social levels. The whites are at the top and the native peoples (Inuit and/or Indians) on the bottom, dependent, and usually living in a physically separate part of town. Inuit and Indians are treated similarly by white agencies, businesses and institutions. This may create a sense of common

Inuit children, like children everywhere, love to play with dolls.

interests between the two groups. The Inuit population of the towns tends to be a conglomerate of several bands which at first lack kinship ties. However, intermarriage is taking place between various Inuit, and sometimes Indian, groups, and new kinship links are developing to replace the traditional ones.

Inuit have been drawn to the towns in search of jobs, schooling, government aid (including medical aid), and in general a better life for themselves and their children. Many came to depend for their livelihood on a combination of work in the towns, government payments and hunting and trapping. This became a new "tradition" for them, arising from their desire to combine aspects of the older way of life with elements of the new. Sometimes only the men go out on the hunting and trapping expeditions. Sometimes, especially in the case of younger families, everybody goes out together into the areas surrounding the settlement.

This type of hunting and trapping cannot supply enough in the way of food and furs to keep a family through the year. But it does keep these families from being entirely dependent on village work or government assistance. It also provides them with a chance to live in a way that is more satisfying to them, a way that keeps them in touch with their ancestral traditions and with the land itself. Many Inuit feel they would like to keep such practices and customs because they continue elements of the old life, as well as providing some food and income. The mixed economy has thus become part of the Inuit way of life.

The Development of Inuit Art

The development of professional and commercial art among the Inuit since the late 1940s has provided another new source of income for many individuals in Inuit villages, particularly in the eastern and central Arctic.

Traditional Inuit art—like most traditional art around the world—was connected with decoration and ornamentation, as well as with religion, worship and aid from the world of spirits, gods and the supernatural. As well, the Inuit took great care in the making of everyday, practical objects—weapons, utensils, toys and so on. In other words, art and craft and music and religion were not sharply divided in the past. Inuit artists did not produce ''art for art's sake.'' They did not think of their works as objects to be placed in art galleries, museums or private art collections.

The Inuit had a long tradition of working in various materials and in three dimensions. They originally carved in ivory, bone or antler. Soapstone, now often thought of as the main material of Inuit sculpture, was used in the past almost exclusively for lamps. (Some Dorset, however, used it for sculpture.) Among some groups, clothing was elaborately decorated with appliqué work and embroidery. The Inuit had no word for ''art,'' but they did have the concept of an object that was well made for its purpose.

The Inuit have always decorated their caribouskin clothing with appliqués and fringes, but it is only since the arrival of the traders that they began to embellish it with intricate beadwork. The elaborate garments seen here would be worn only on special occasions.

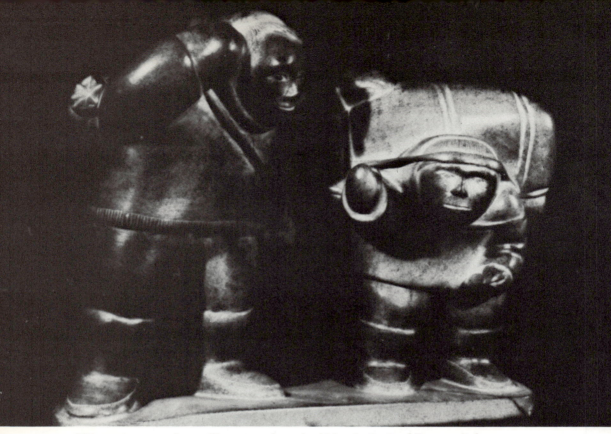

This soapstone sculpture illustrates a legend told by the Inuit of Povungnituk, Quebec, about an encounter between a man hunting for caribou and a dwarf. The dwarf, who is carrying a big male caribou on his back, is pointing out the way the hunter must follow in order to find what he is looking for.

With the coming of the European whalers and explorers, the Inuit found that they could trade or sell some of the objects they made as souvenirs. After a while, they began to make carvings, mainly of animal and human figures, specifically for this purpose. The market was not great, but it grew as more fur traders, missionaries and others came into the North. Inuit skills in making objects have continued to the present day, except perhaps on the Labrador coast, but until the mid-twentieth century, the objects made were thought of mainly as souvenirs.

The development of Inuit art is the result of a combination of traditional and new elements contributed by the Inuit, plus a new way of thinking about Inuit work on the part of outsiders. In the first half of the twentieth century, artistic tastes began to expand to include an acceptance of different world art traditions. Objects made by native inhabitants of southern North America, the south Pacific and Africa, once of interest only to souvenir hunters and anthropologists, began to be appreciated as art. In a similar way, people began to appreciate the art of the Inuit.

Art as a Source of Income
During the first half of the twentieth century, a few efforts were made to find markets for Inuit art in order to create income. It was not until 1948 that a major breakthrough came.

That year, a representative of the Canadian Handicraft Guild, James Houston, visited Port Harrison and saw the Inuit work there. He became very excited about it, especially the soapstone work. He encouraged the Inuit to do more work, and to depict subjects that would be of interest to collectors.

The first major show of Inuit sculpture took place in 1949. About a thousand pieces were exhibited. The show was to last for a week, but everything sold in three days! The Canadian Handicraft Guild purchased more Inuit artwork and had sold more than eleven thousand pieces by 1951. Encouraged by the awakening interest and demand, Inuit artists soon emerged in many villages.

In recent years the Inuit have produced brilliant carvings of stone, whalebone, ivory and antler. They have broadened the scope of their appliqué and embroidery skills to work with a variety of textiles, and they have acquired new skills in print-making (stencils, engraving, stone-cuts and silk-screen). The first prints were formally exhibited between 1957 and 1959. Today, print-making is among the most important artistic activities of the Inuit.

At the start, the Inuit had help from outsiders and suggestions about types of art that would sell and how to sell them. However, they quickly took over much of the management of their own art industry. The first Inuit artists' co-operative was formed in 1959. Through co-ops, the Inuit control their own work and judge its quality. In recent years, the work has been aimed at art collectors rather than at the souvenir market. Inuit organizations guarantee the authenticity of a work by marking and stamping it with the name of the artist and the area in which he or she lives. They keep track of the number of objects produced and in certain cases—especially with prints—limit the number. The Inuit have thus made another adaptation to the commercial outside world. They have fitted an aspect of their culture—their arts and crafts—to the interests of the dominant culture to the south. At the same time they have gradually reintroduced traditional subjects, including religious subjects, into their art. Spirit beings and traditional stories are now represented in contrast to the earlier tendency to portray primarily everyday life and only human and animal figures.

During the late 1940s and 1950s, individual Inuit artists were not well known. More recently the distinctive talents of particular artists has come to be appreciated and many Inuit artists have acquired national and international reputations. Some of the most famous designers of stone-cuts have come from Cape Dorset. They include Kenojuak, Lucy, Pitseolak, and Pudlo. The community of Povungnituk has produced Joe Talirunili and others. Jessie Oonark of Baker Lake has achieved wide recognition for her felt wall hangings with their elaborate and colourful embroidery. Works of sculpture have come from artists in many villages across the North.

Inuit art has shown non-native people the creativity and artistic skills of the Inuit. It has also fostered a sense of self-awareness and vitality among the Inuit themselves. It is part of what has been called a ''renaissance'' or rebirth and of the Inuit's movement to regain control over their own lives and culture. Regaining this control means gaining a degree of economic independence. It means building a society that can adapt to change without giving up what is good and meaningful from the traditions of the past.

Co-operative Action as a Means Towards Self-Government

As a means of further increasing their control over their own af-

Inuit children at school in the Northwest Territories.

fairs, the Inuit have created co-operatives to deal with aspects of their lives other than arts and crafts. The first of these co-operatives was formed in 1959. Encouraged by the federal government, the co-ops aimed to promote economic development leading to greater independence and a higher standard of living. As a first step towards achieving this, production, buying and selling were to be placed in Inuit control.

Co-ops spread quickly and were eventually created to deal with a wide variety of economic activities—arts and crafts, fishing, fur trading, tourism, retail trade, service industries. Where they serve a variety of needs they tend to be more important in the community than where they serve only one or two. They have also become a kind of adult education centre. Their members, through lectures, discussions and experience, receive training in

Except in isolated communities, snowmobiles have largely replaced the dogsled as the main means of winter transportation in the North.

marketing, accounting, management and other aspects of business administration. Participants can develop skills in public speaking and organizational leadership. In these ways, the co-ops offer a variety of learning experiences and have an impact beyond their specific concerns.

The co-ops have led to greater contact between communities as delegates meet at conferences to learn from each other. They have helped to bind together individuals and communities previously divided by ethnic and/or religious differences. Protestants and Roman Catholics, Inuit, Indians, Métis and white, or some combination of these, have often begun working together as a direct result of co-op membership.

Co-ops have also helped bridge differences which were growing up between various aspects of the economy. Those who hunted and fished for a livelihood, for example, were expected, as they had always been, to share their catch with others. On the other hand, those who earned a living in the village in new occupations were not expected to share their earnings. Not surprisingly, this created problems. By incorporating the economic activities and needs of both elements within the co-ops it was possible to achieve a solution.

Co-ops are a local, community-sized approach to economic and social needs. They have tried to deal efficiently with the exploitation of the resources, wildlife and human, available in the settlements. In this way they contrast with economic and technological projects which originate in Ottawa or in the great industrial and financial centres of Canada or other countries. These projects, such as vast hydro-electric and mining schemes, are planned and managed from outside the Inuit communities. The Inuit have little or no control over them and the potential changes which they could bring about. Although the framework of the modern co-operative was also introduced by non-Inuit, co-ops have tried to end the Inuit's sense of dependency and lack of control over their own affairs. Some Inuit see these organizations as the modern form of the old camp-life custom of sharing and group decision making.

The James Bay Agreement

In the early 1970s the Quebec government wanted to acquire Inuit and Indian land on the eastern shore of James Bay for a massive hydro-electric project. An agreement was worked out and concluded in 1975 between the government and the Inuit and Cree Indians of the area. It was negotiated on the Inuit side by Charlie Watt of Fort Chimo, president of the North Quebec Inuit Association.

Under the terms of the agreement, the Inuit surrendered their rights to most of the land in return for cash compensation and the division of the land into three categories. Category One was land assigned to the native peoples exclusively. This amounted to 8400 square kilometres. No development was permitted in this area without native consent. Category Two land allowed Inuit to retain hunting, fishing and trapping rights. Under this category, the Inuit were given 90,700 square kilometres for their use. Any development on the land by industry and government entitled the Inuit to compensation. Category Three land also allowed the Inuit hunting, fishing and trapping rights, but these rights were subject to cancellation at any time and without compensation.

Inuit in the Northwest Territories, unlike the James Bay Inuit, vowed that they did not want and would not accept such a settlement. There, slogans such as "This Land is Not for Sale" and "No Once-for-All Settlement" began to be heard.

Inuit Organizations and Land Claims

During the 1970s Inuit organizations sprang into existence at both the national and regional levels. The aim of such organizations was to shape Inuit opinion, to formulate it more clearly and to make plans for dealing with what the Inuit increasingly interpreted as a threat to their land, their way of life, their values and traditions.

The Inuit Tapirisat

In 1971 the Inuit Tapirisat of Canada (ITC) was formed. Its main purpose was to represent all Inuit in land claims dealings with the federal government. In general terms, the ITC is dedicated to preserving the culture, identity and way of life of the Inuit, and to helping them find their role in a changing society.

The Inuit Tapirisat submitted a claim to Ottawa for 650,000 square kilometres of land and water in the Northwest Territories and rights to minerals down to 457 metres below the surface. It also asked for the right to choose the area that would be included in this land settlement. The Inuit base their claim on aboriginal title and the historical fact that they have neither signed away their land by treaties nor been conquered in war. Aboriginal rights, they assert, are the property rights of native people in the land they have traditionally used and occupied "from time immemorial." According to an Inuit land claim of 1978, this prior occupancy gives them the right to determine how things are done in their lands, to be a significant part of the decision-making pro-

The one-hand reach, one of the events at the Arctic Winter Games. The Games have been held every two years since 1970 and are specifically designed for people living north of the sixtieth parallel.

cess in resource development, to benefit from what might be exported from the North and to exercise a degree of control over the political-constitutional processes that will determine their future.

In 1975 the ITC urged the creation of a new territorial government in the Northwest Territories. This new government was to have jurisdiction over the entire area subject to Inuit land claims. The territory would be called Nunavut (Our Land). It would be north of the tree line, the traditional boundary of Inuit country. The main responsibility of Inuit territorial government would be to develop—in cooperation with the federal govern-

Arctic Shorebirds, *a Cape Dorset print by Luktak.*

ment—programs for educational, social and economic development.

The Inuit territorial government would also protect Inuit culture, manage wildlife and the environment, and control mineral development. In 1976 James Arvaluk, commenting on Inuit history, stated: "Ours is a forgotten colony . . . . We are seldom if ever consulted *before* . . . decisions are made. Instead we are informed *after* the fact . . . . But we don't want to be colonial subjects . . . . We want to be *partners* in Confederation."

The Inuit land claim became an issue—perhaps the major public issue—in Inuit affairs in the 1970s and early 1980s. The land issue is closely linked to culture survival and future growth. This is reflected in a booklet published in January 1978 by the Northwest Territories Inuit Land Claims Commission. The booklet is titled *Inuit Nunangat—The People's Land: A Struggle for Survival*. The Inuit can look only to themselves for protection, it asserts. They are faced with the task of rebuilding and developing a new life after near extinction due to colonization by southern Canada. The Inuit, it is proposed, want Canada to agree to certain rights of the Inuit:

> the right to self-determination
> the right to own their traditional lands and waters, including the subsurface
> the right to practise and preserve their language and culture
> the right to preserve and exercise their traditional hunting, trapping and fishing rights
> the right to define who is an Inuk
> the right to exist as an independent culture within Canada

Several regional organizations were formed in the mid-1970s to join with the national organization, the ITC, to protect, defend and promote the interests and plans of the Inuit: the Baffin Region Inuit Association, the Keewatin Inuit Association, the Labrador Inuit Association, the Northern Quebec Inuit Association, and the Committee for Original Peoples Entitlement (COPE) representing the Inuit of the Mackenzie River delta.

The Berger Inquiry

In the mid-1970s, the federal government appointed Justice Thomas Berger to examine and report on the effects of a 1972 proposal to build a natural gas pipeline in the Mackenzie River valley. Social, environmental and economic effects were investigated, and testimony was taken from groups and individuals, including Inuit and other native people. Much of the information gathered was technical and scientific, but many people also told Justice Berger about their lives, their values and customs, and their desire to protect their way of life, the land and the wildlife. A man from Aklavik expressed an Inuit view of land and lifestyle in the following words:

> In many ways I inherit what my grandfather and my father have given to me; a place to live in, a place to own, something I have a right to . . . I would like to give something for the future generation of my children, so they also should have a right to inherit this country.

As a result of the Berger inquiry, the pipeline was delayed and public awareness—both native and non-native—was greatly increased and stimulated.

The Territorial Council

Because most of Canada's Inuit live in the Northwest Territories, the convening in May 1975 of the first fully elected Territorial Council was an important event for them. Since that time the majority of territorial representatives have been natives—Inuit, Indians and Métis. In 1980 Peter Ittinuar became the first Inuk elected to the federal Parliament in Ottawa.

The work of Inuit local, regional and national organizations has been aided and supported by Inuit and others who were elected to the Territorial Council from electoral constituencies where Inuit form the majority of the population.

The Inuit Look to Tomorrow . . .
and Remember Yesterday

In order to deal with their many different needs and desires, the

Inuit are forming organizations and plans that will give them greater control over both their near and distant future. Political and economic activity are at the forefront. Control and management of the land and its resources—non-renewable and renewable—are key issues. But these are only part of what concerns the Inuit, an aspect of the larger subject of Inuit cultural growth and development.

The Inuit want to grow and develop without losing what they see as valuable from the past. Those elements of their past that are worth retaining, they wish to retain and take with them into the future, though perhaps in modified and adapted form. The preservation, or in some places the revival, of the language is very important. Control of education and the shaping of courses of study for Inuit children in the North are subjects of immediate importance. Through local government such matters can be dealt with. What emerges then is a variety of issues and concerns, all interrelated, ranging from Inuit-run investment corporations to the annual Inuit northern games. No topic can be handled singly. All seem to require attention at the same time. The Inuit Tapirisat of Canada has answered the question, "What do the Inuit want?":

> [They] . . . want the opportunity to run their own affairs.
> What the Inuit want is not really much different from
> what most Canadians already take for granted.

In a speech called "Canada's Forgotten Colony" James Arvaluk gave this summary of the Inuit past since the coming of the first Europeans and of the present and future as the Inuit see them.

> White southern society has never really cared about our land as such. From the beginning, the intruders have come there either by mistake, or were drawn by what they could get out of it. But seldom to stay, to live in it, to be a part of it. The early explorers were the first intruders. They were looking for a shortcut to the Orient. Then came the whalers. Then the fur traders, who began the process of teaching the Eskimos to live in settlements— not to enhance the well-being of the native people, but to enhance the profits of the trading companies. The mis-

sionaries, mounties and the government administrators followed, compelled by what is sometimes called the White man's burden. The prospectors and the dew-liners came along determined to make a fast buck and get back to "civilization" as quickly as possible. And now there's a new breed of explorer looking for oil, natural gas, mineral wealth under the ground . . . and for the first time we feel our land is threatened. The Inuit have awakened to the realization that we must act together to preserve and protect our territory, our culture, our identity . . . . Like it or not, we are being forced into 20th century western civilization, and it becomes clear that if we don't look after our own interests, no one will. And what are those interests we want to protect? To put it into the simplest terms, the Inuit want a voice in running their own affairs.

Selected Biographies

CURLEY, Tagak

Tagak Curley is one of the best known figures in Inuit public life. In 1971 he founded and became first president of the national Inuit organization, the Inuit Tapirisat of Canada.

Like other Inuit public figures, Curley has had a variety of work experiences in Inuit communities and organizations. He has encouraged the creation of various kinds of Inuit activities and taken a leading role in their development. He has been Executive Director of the Inuit Cultural Institute and was president of the Inuit Development Corporation. He serves as a member of the Legislative Assembly of the Northwest Territories, one of several Inuit in that body.

Tagak Curley has tried in a variety of ways to understand the workings of Canadian society, its organizations and structures, so that the Inuit may deal more effectively with them. From his experience he has concluded that mastering the techniques of non-Inuit society requires management, organization and discipline.

ITTINUAR, Peter

Peter Ittinuar is the first and only Inuk to become a member of Canada's Parliament. Elected in May 1979, he sits for the riding of Nunatsiaq, the northeastern area of the Northwest Territories and the largest riding in Canada.

Ittinuar was born and raised in Rankin Inlet. He has worked as a translator, lectured at the University of Ottawa and been a bush pilot. In addition, he has worked as a photographer and film-maker, producing educational material and articles for the magazine *Inuit Monthly*. For a time he was a Director of the Inuit Tapirisat of Canada.

A member of the New Democratic Party, Ittinuar acts as that party's parliamentary critic for northern development. His maiden speech in Parliament was another first: he delivered it in Inuktitut.

KENOJUAK

Kenojuak is one of Canada's most renowned and respected artists. She was born in 1927 at Ikarasak and grew up travelling from camp to camp in northern Quebec and on southern Baffin Island.

While living near Cape Dorset in 1957, Kenojuak and her husband Jonniebo began to draw and to carve in soapstone. Her first print, *Rabbit Eating Seaweed*, was made in 1958, and the first exhibit of her work was held the following year. Since then she has continued to exhibit in galleries throughout Canada and in other countries. Her works have been used on postage stamps and represented many times in books, illustrated catalogues and other printed material. In 1961 the National Film Board made a film about her life and art. She was awarded the Order of Canada in 1967 and in 1970 travelled with her husband to an exhibition of her work in Osaka, Japan.

Enchanted Owl is perhaps the most famous Inuit work of art, and is typical in its design of the fantastic birds and other animals which make Kenojuak's work distinctive. In 1981 a special limited edition book of her works was published. She has had ten children most of whom died in childhood.

Kenojuak has been called the "luminary" of Inuit artists.

LUCY

Lucy, who was born about 1915, had eleven children, including two that were adopted. Most of her children died before reaching adulthood. In the mid-1960s she moved to Cape Dorset, where she met James and Alma Houston and began to do drawings. Her subjects were imaginary birds, flowers and people. Many of her works have a fantastic and playful appearance. Her work has been collected in a number of galleries, including the Tate Gallery in London. One of her earliest works was *Family Startled by Goose* (1960). She has been a very productive artist.

OONARK, Jessie

Jessie Oonark was born in 1906 in the Back River area of the Northwest Territories. She married and has had eight children and almost fifty grandchildren. In 1959, after her husband died, she settled with her family in Baker Lake.

Oonark's talent was first recognized by a non-Inuit scientist who encouraged her to work on paper as well as cloth. She worked steadily adding to her accomplishments, and has created designs for special stamps and for large textile wall hangings. A wall hanging by Oonark was presented to the Queen in 1973. Another decorates the office of the Prime Minister of Canada.

Her work has been exhibited across Canada in galleries and museums. The figures include birds, animals and humans. One of her favourite techniques is to sketch figures onto woollen material and then cut them out and sew them onto a large hanging, so that they are cloth pictures. Often the design contains a pattern formed by images of ulus.

Like Kenojuak and others among the Inuit artists, Oonark speaks only Inuktitut.

PITSEOLAK

Pitseolak, born in 1904, married Ashoona. She had seventeen children, though most died in childhood. The surviving children are themselves artists. In the early 1960s, after her husband died, Pitseolak moved permanently to Cape Dorset. Some of her art shows daily life and everyday scenes of the Inuit. Others of her works are of fantastic animals and scenes from imagination and legends. Her work is represented in the National Gallery of Canada, and she is a member of the Royal Canadian Academy of Arts. In 1977 she became the second Cape Dorset artist to be given the Order of Canada in recognition of her artistic contribution to the country.

Pitseolak's autobiography *Pictures Out of My Life* was published in 1971.

PUDLO (Padluk Pudlat)
Pudlo was born near Kamadjuak in 1916. He has been married three times. Most of his children died in childhood. The family settled at Cape Dorset where Pudlo became part of the artist community.

Pudlo did not begin to draw until the 1950s. Later he expanded his creative activities to include painting and sculpture. Some of his most famous works include *Caribou Tent* (1973), *Ecclesiast* (1969) and *Man Carrying Reluctant Wife* (1961). Many of his works have a humorous and happy subject. Since 1961 he has exhibited widely in the United States and Europe as well as in Canada. His work has also been used on Canadian postage stamps.

Many galleries and private collectors have Pudlo's works in their collections.

WATT, Charlie
Charlie Watt was born in 1944 in Fort Chimo, one of fifteen Inuit communities in northern Quebec. He attended school in Churchill and Ottawa and has worked for the Department of Indian Affairs and Northern Development.

Watt became active in Quebec Inuit public life in the 1970s mainly because of his opposition to the original proposal for the James Bay project. He organized the Northern Quebec Inuit Association to lobby against it and as president of the association negotiated terms more favourable to the Inuit. From 1979 to 1982 he was president of Makivik, a development corporation set up to "administer and implement the terms and monies flowing from the James Bay agreement."

While working for the Department of Indian Affairs, Watt came to feel that the Inuit had become far too dependent on the government for employment, health care and education. He was convinced that the situation must change and that the Inuit must develop a broader economic base by involving themselves in the development of their lands' resources.

In the late 1970s, Charlie Watt became interested in the constitutional process and with Tagak Curley formed the Inuit Committee on National Issues.

Glossary

Aboriginal   Relating to the earliest known inhabitants of a place. "Aboriginal rights" refer to the right of native people to the lands they occupied before the establishment of the Dominion of Canada.

Angakok   Shaman—he or she controls supernatural forces to aid in healing and hunting and may also use their powers to hurt or injure.

Archaeologist   A scientist who searches for and studies material evidence remaining from human life and culture in past ages.

Artifact   An object made by human workmanship, and particularly one such as a simple tool, weapon or ornament which is of archaelogical or historical interest.

Baleen   Elastic, horny material that grows in place of teeth in the upper jaw of certain whales. Also known as whalebone.

Barren Grounds   The region of northern Canada that lies between Hudson Bay and Great Slave Lake. Although it is called "barren," much of it is covered in summer by small flowering plants, lichen, grass and shrubs.

Co-operative   An organization owned and directed by the membership to make and market products and in which the profits are shared by the membership.

Culture   The way of life of a people. It includes everything a group of people has, makes, thinks, believes and passes on to its children.

Dorset   The name archaeologists give to the people who inhabited the Canadian Arctic between about 800 B.C. and A.D. 1000.

Igloo   An Inuit house made of ice blocks, used for winter housing.

Inuit   The Inuit's name for themselves, the People.

Inuit Tapirisat of Canada   The national Inuit organization.

Inuk   A person.

Inukshuk   A pile of large stones arranged to roughly resemble a human figure. Used to hunt cariboo and guide travellers.

Inuktitut   The language of the Inuit.

Kayak   A skin boat for a single person, used mainly for hunting and to some extent for travel.

Komatik   Inuit dogsled.

Kudlik   Soapstone lamp in which the Inuit burned seal, whale or caribou oil.

Leister   Two- or three-pronged fishing spear with a long handle.

Lichen   A flowerless plant resembling moss that grows in patches on rocks and trees.

Nunavut   "Our land." A portion of the eastern Northwest Territories proposed as an Inuit homeland.

Permafrost   A condition of permanently frozen earth.

Polynya   An area of water never completely frozen which attracts a variety of wildlife and is therefore ideal for hunting.

Sedna   Goddess of the sea from whose fingers sea life was formed.

Soapstone   A heavy stone that feels somewhat like soap. Also called steatite.

Syllabary   A writing system in which the characters represent syllables.

Thule   The ancestors of the Inuit. They moved eastward out of Alaska starting about A.D. 1000 and gradually displaced the Dorset.

Tundra   The vast "treeless" plains of the Arctic region.

Tunit   The Inuit name for pre-Inuit people of the Arctic.

Tupik   A skin tent, the summer dwelling of the Inuit.

Ulu   A woman's crescent-shaped bone knife.

Umiak   A large, open skin boat used for transportation of people and goods and for whaling.

Weir   A fence of rocks built across a stream to catch fish.

Whiteout   A weather condition occurring in the Arctic when the sky is overcast. The cloudy sky and the snow-covered ground merge into a shadowless, dazzling whiteness, the horizon disappears and only very dark objects can be seen.

Eskimo — Inuit

The native peoples of northern North America have long been known as Eskimos. In recent times, however, the northern peoples of Canada have rejected the term Eskimo. It was originally an Indian term meaning "Eaters of raw meat" and considered derogatory. The term Inuit, meaning "The People," is now used to refer to the northern native peoples of Canada. "Eskimo" is accepted by the northern native peoples living in Alaska.

Selected Further Reading

Cowan, Susan, ed. *We Don't Live in Snow Houses Now:* Reflections from Arctic Bay. Ottawa: Canadian Arctic producers, 1976. First-person accounts of life in modern Inuit settlements with numerous illustrations.

French, Alice. *My Name is Masak.* Winnipeg: Peguis Publishers, 1976. A simply written autobiographical account of growing up in the Western Arctic before World War II and of the divided loyalties caused by the conflicting influences of Inuit and white societies.

Harrington, Richard. *The Inuit: Life As It Was.* Edmonton: Hurtig, 1981. One hundred and fifty wonderfully evocative photographs accompanied by a text that is at once simple, informative and moving.

Larmour, W. T. *Inunnit: The Art of the Canadian Eskimo.* Ottawa: Department of Indian Affairs and Northern Development, 1967. Over a hundred examples of Inuit sculpture and graphic art.

McGhee, Robert. *Canadian Arctic Prehistory.* Ottawa: National Museum of Man, 1978. On the basis of archaeological discoveries, the author reconstructs the life of the pre-Inuit inhabitants of the North. Clearly written and attractively illustrated.

————— *The Tunit: First Explorers of the High Arctic.* Ottawa: National Museum of Man, 1981. This book is written in two parts, one a fictional account of the daily lives of the Tunit, the other a description of the archaeological information on which the author's imaginative reconstruction is based.

Metayer, Maurice. *Tales from the Igloo.* Edmonton: Hurtig, 1972. Stories, legends and fables of the Copper Inuit, illustrated by Nanogak, an Inuit artist.

North/Nord Ottawa: Department of Indian Affairs and Northern Development. A well-illustrated and informative bi-monthly magazine.

Nuligak. *I, Nuligak,* translated from Inuktitut by Maurice Metayer. Markham: PaperJacks, 1971. The first published autobiography of an Inuk.

Pitseolak. *Pictures Out of My Life.* Toronto: Oxford University Press, 1971. The artist's autobiography, edited from tape-recorded interviews by Dorothy Weber. Illustrated with Pitseolak's own sketches and prints.

Stories from Pangnirtung. Edmonton: Hurtig, 1976. The simply-told recollections of the elders of a Baffin Island community, translated from tape-recorded interviews. Illustrated by Germain Arnauktauyak.

Tagoona, Armand. *Shadows.* Ottawa: Oberon Press, 1975. Twenty-three drawings with an explanatory text describing traditions, legends and the author's life as hunter, priest and artist.

For Discussion

INTRODUCTION

1) Make a bar graph comparing the temperature in your town with that in one or two northern communities. If possible do this for different times of year. Are the results what you would have expected?
2) What is permafrost? Consult an encyclopedia and write a short essay on the practical problems this condition creates.
3) What is the tundra? Is it completely accurate to call it treeless? If not, why do we do so?
4) Make a list of things you see or use every day that are made of wood. Would it be possible to make them all in some other material? If so, would it be easier or more difficult to make them? To use them? If not, how would not having them affect your life?
5) How many English words meaning "snow" can you think of? Inuktitut has well over a dozen. Can you imagine why?

CHAPTER 1

1) Where did the earliest inhabitants of the Canadian Arctic come from?
2) How do we know what areas the Pre-Dorset and Dorset people occupied?
3) Why did these peoples and those who followed them keep moving from place to place? How did they decide where to locate their camps or villages?
4) What was the most important tool/weapon of the Pre-Dorset? Why is it important to archaeologists?
5) The seal was probably the most important resource of the Dorset. Why?
6) Write a paragraph on the religious beliefs of the Dorset.
7) What is thought to have caused the disappearance of the Dorset?
8) No one knows for sure why the forerunners of the Inuit chose to stay in harsh northern lands instead of moving south to a kinder climate as the ancestors of the Indians had done. Can you suggest any reasons?

CHAPTER 2

1) In what main ways did the Thule lifestyle differ from that of the people who came earlier?
2) What uses other than food did the Thule make of the whale?
3) Most early societies used wood and bark as fuel and for making dwellings, boats, bows and arrows and other necessities. What did the northern people use instead?
4) Why is it necessary to say that the Thule were *probably* the first Arctic people to meet Europeans?
5) Although the Thule are the ancestors of the Inuit we talk about them as having distinct "cultures." What change in their way of life causes us to

make this distinction? What brought about this change? Did it happen suddenly?

6) Read about the arrival of the first Europeans in some other part of the world (southern Canada, Mexico, Africa, for instance). Compare the events and developments with those which occurred in northern Canada. In what ways are they similar? different?

CHAPTER 3

1) Why were co-operation and sharing so important in Inuit life? Give examples of the survival value of these traits.
2) In what ways did the Inuit live off the land for food? clothing? utensils? fuel? housing? other things?
3) Why was story-telling an important feature of Inuit life?
4) Name the nine Inuit subgroups.
5) Describe one way of seal or caribou hunting.
6) In what way did the Caribou Inuit live differently from other groups?
7) How did the regular coming of the whalers affect the Inuit? Why did they eventually stop coming?
8) What main church groups sent missionaries to the Arctic? What was their primary purpose?
9) Why was the introduction of a writing system important to the preservation of Inuit culture?
10) Do you think the Inuit were better or worse off as a result of the presence of the missionaries? Justify your answer.
11) How do you suppose the whalers and the Inuit communicated with each other the first times they met? Act out such a meeting.
12) Do you think that their way of life made the Inuit more or less "free" than the city or country Canadians in the South? Explain.

CHAPTER 4

1) What was the standard of the Inuit fur trade?
2) What articles did the Inuit most want from the traders?
3) How did the fur trade affect Inuit-Indian relations?
4) Why did many Inuit become dependent on outsiders for tools, weapons, food and clothes? How did this affect their way of life and their well-being?
5) Why did traders and missionaries sometimes come into conflict?
6) What role did the RCMP play in the North during the early 1900s?
7) What could the traders, missionaries and other Europeans learn from the Inuit?
8) Suggest reasons for the failure of the government's efforts to introduce reindeer herding among the Inuit.
9) Describe a typical trading scene at a Hudson's Bay Company post.
10) How did Inuit-European contact affect the size and distribution of Inuit population? Explain why and give examples.

CHAPTER 5

1) Explain three ways in which Inuit communities changed after World War II.
2) Why was the government of Canada so uninterested in the North for so long? When did this change and why?
3) What has the development of Inuit art meant in practical terms for the Inuit? in other ways?
4) Explain the role of co-operatives.
5) Find out more about one of the Inuit organizations mentioned in this chapter and write a brief report on its aims and accomplishments.
6) Read some Inuit legends. Do you find any special concern about food? rivalry? co-operation? success? relation to nature? importance of technology? helpful or harmful supernatural beings or forces?
7) If you had been able to vote in the 1982 plebiscite on the creation of Nunavut, how would you have voted? Why? Do you think you would have voted the same way if you were an Inuit or a non-Inuit living in the area?
8) Try to imagine a province of Nunavut. What would be some of its concerns and problems?
9) Why do the Inuit reject the term "Eskimo" and use the name "Inuit"? What is in a name?

Index